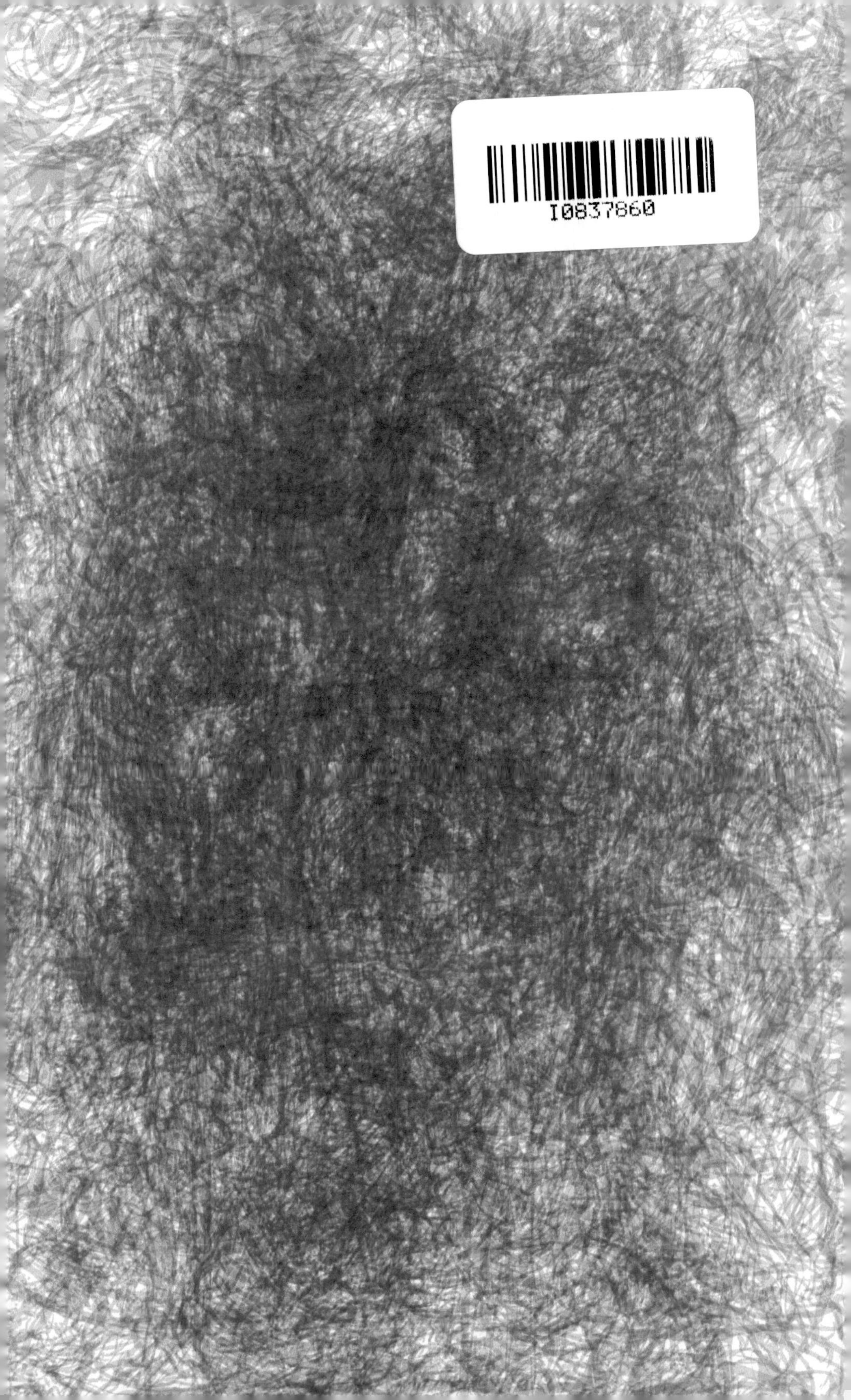

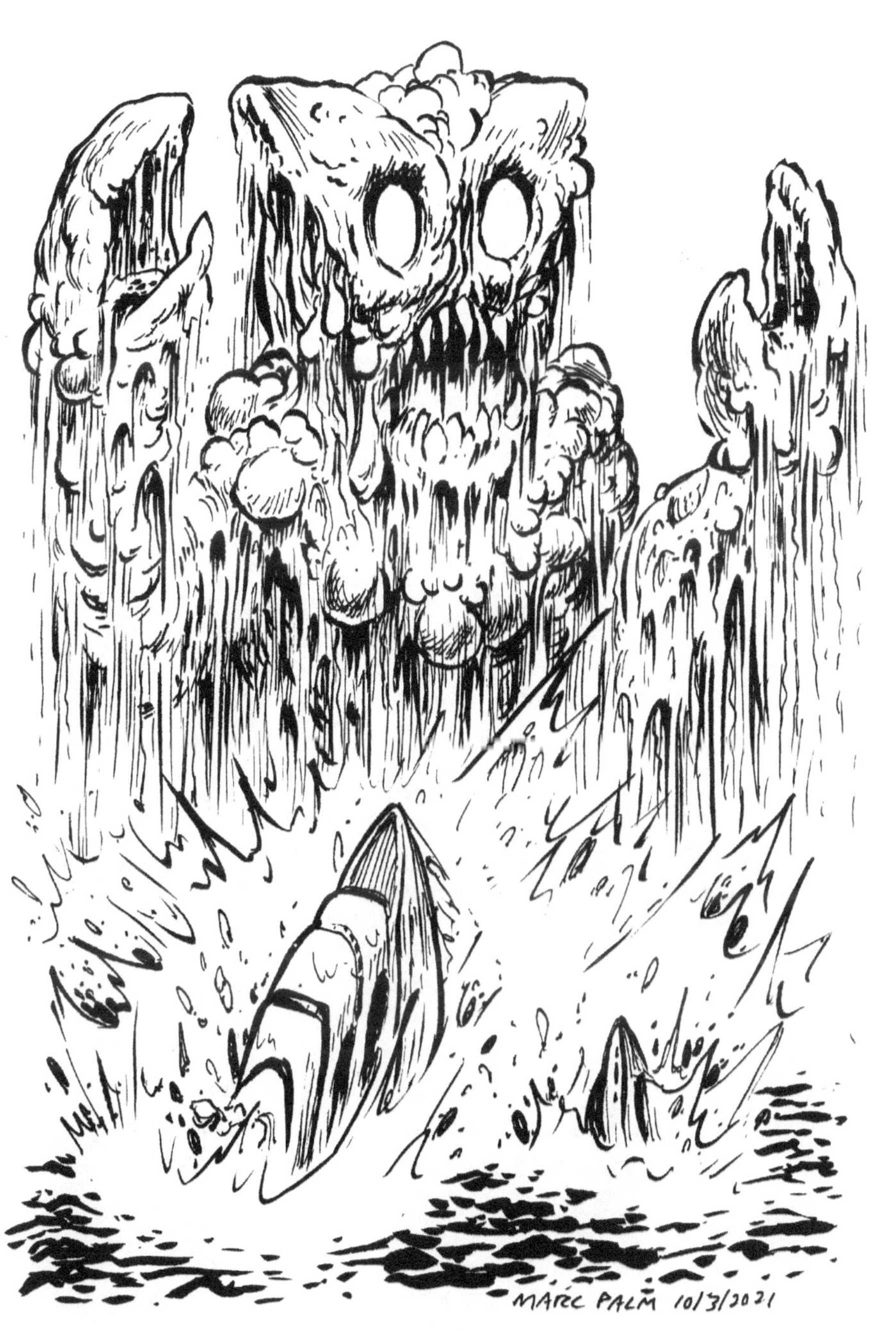
MARC PALM 10/3/2021

MUTATED MONSTERS 31 ILLUSTRATIONS

Marc Palm's Mutated Monsters - 31 Illustrations
ink and pencil on backing board created between 9/2 - 10/31

All artwork contained within is copyright 2021 Marc Palm / Self Satisfied Books
ISBN: 978-1-7947-8500-7   Imprint: Lulu.com

E-mail for permissions or questions - swellzombie@gmail.com   IG - marcjpalm
This is a Self Satisifed Production - Thank you to the 24 people who commissioned individual pieces and allowed me to "live the dream". Thank you to my patrons for the support.

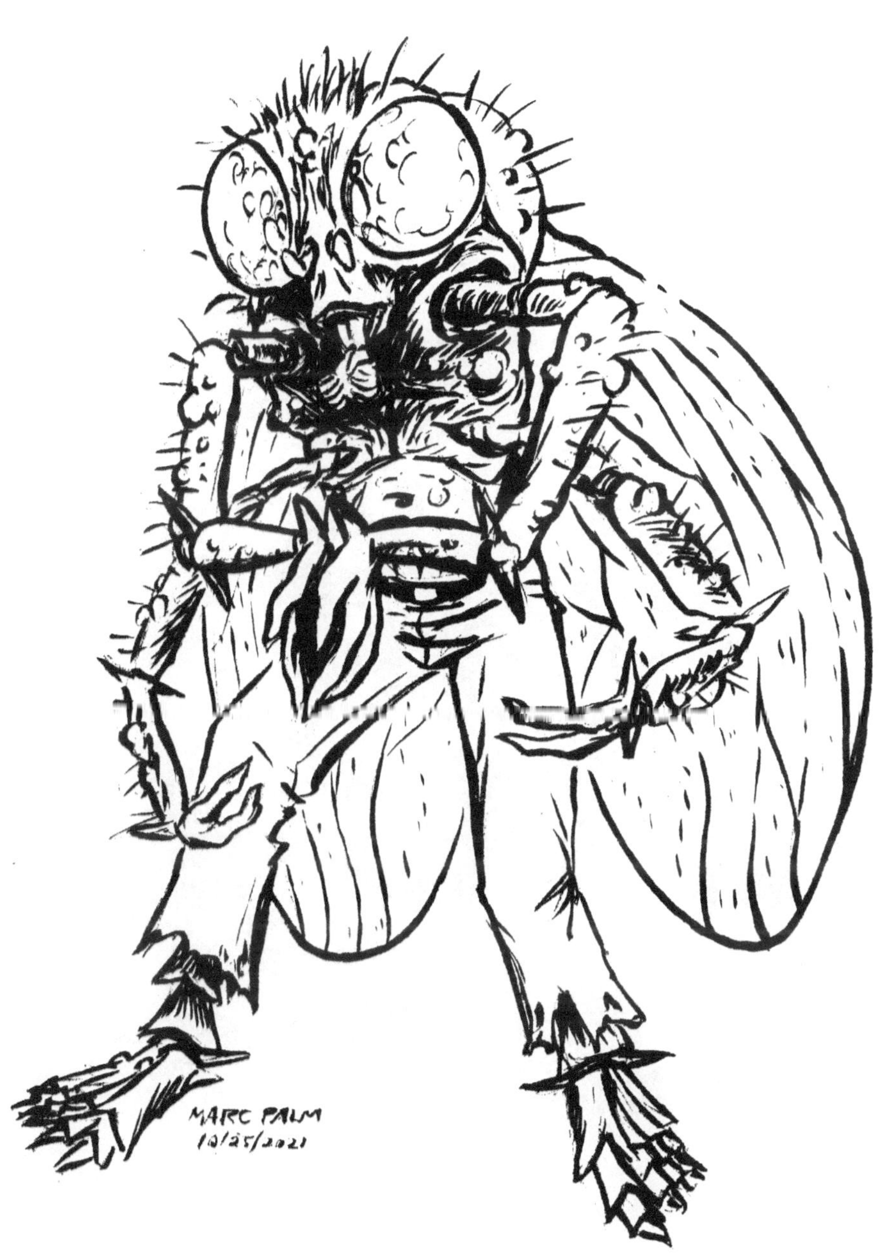
MARC PALM
10/25/2021

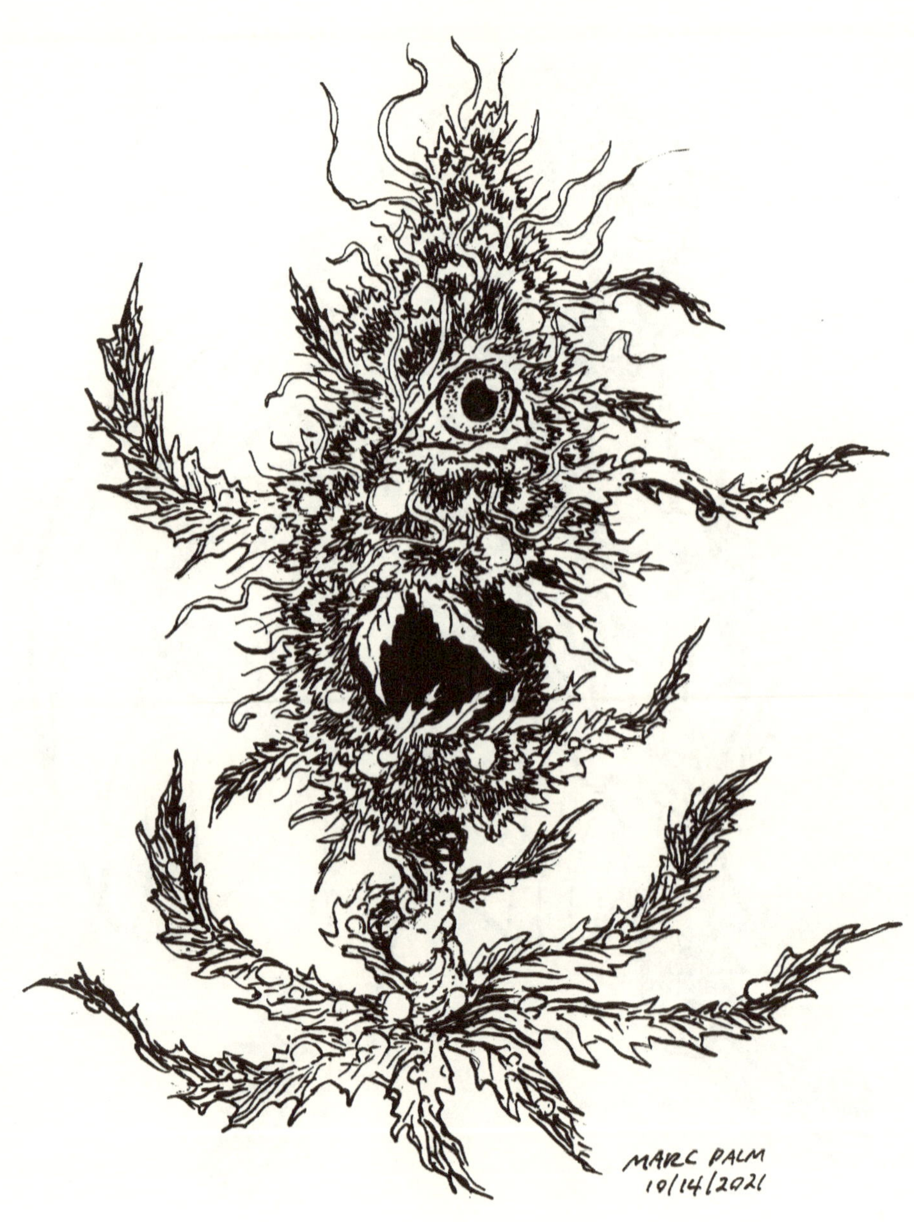

MARC PALM
10/14/2021

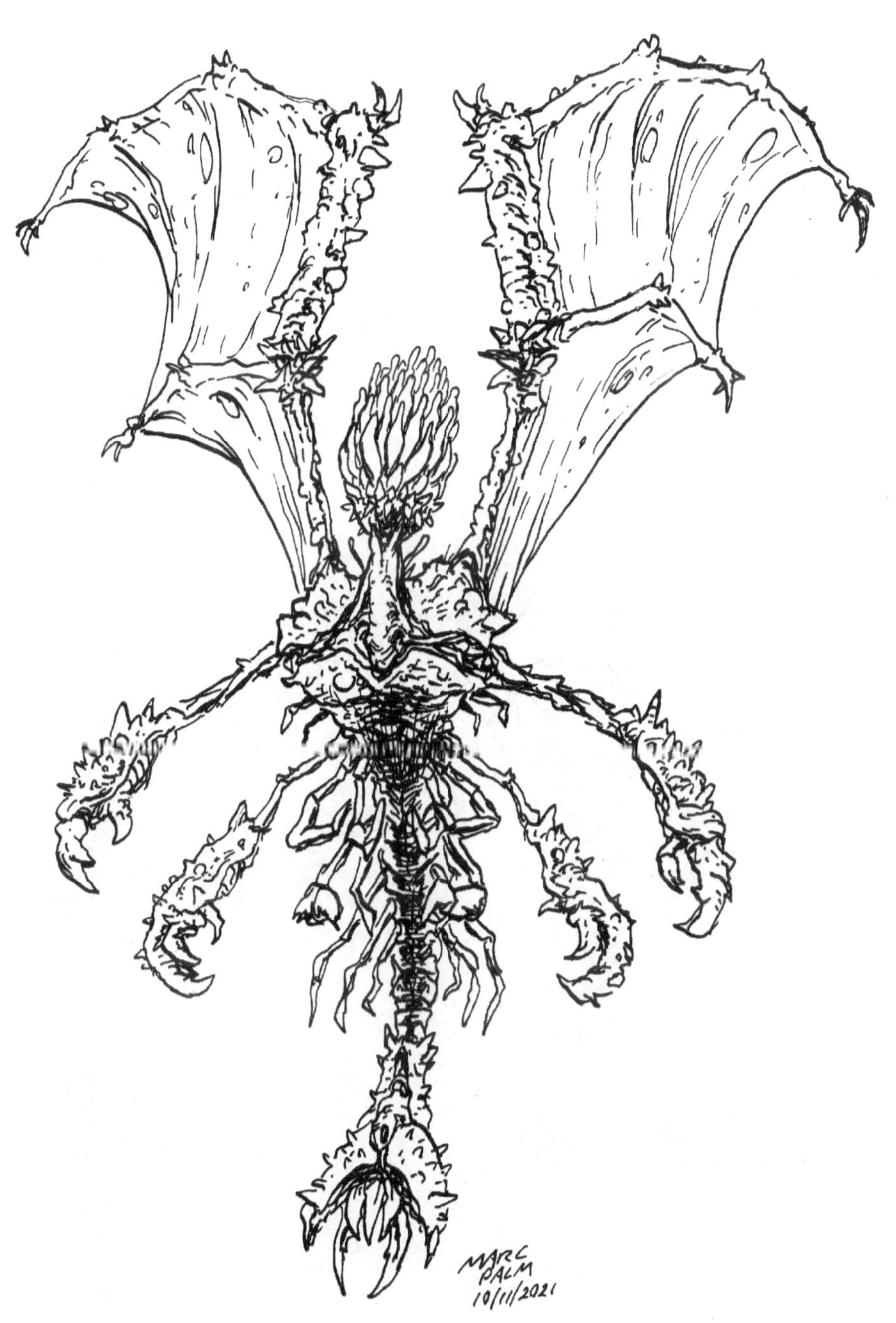

MARC
PALM
10/11/2021

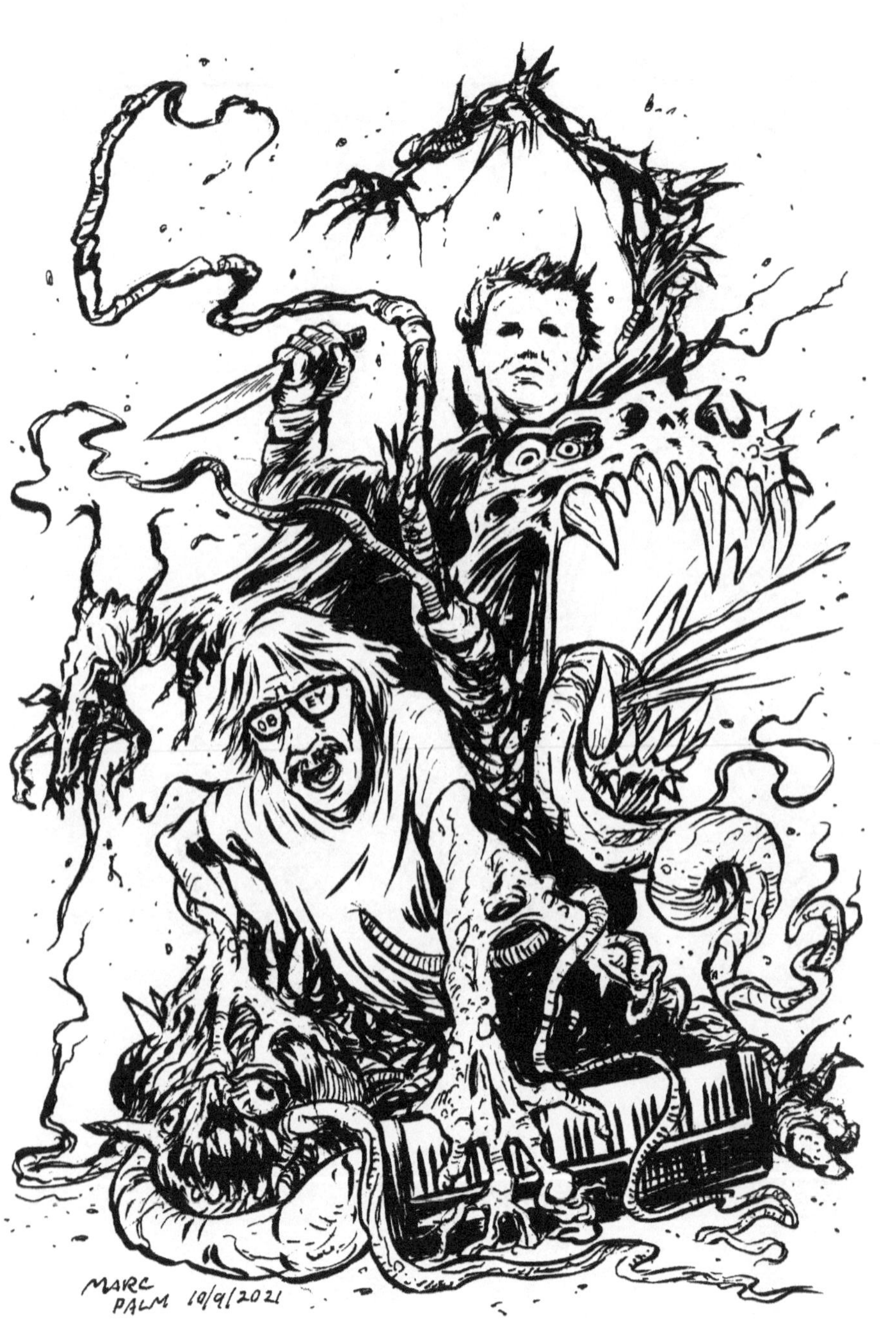

OBEY
MARC
PALM 10/9/2021

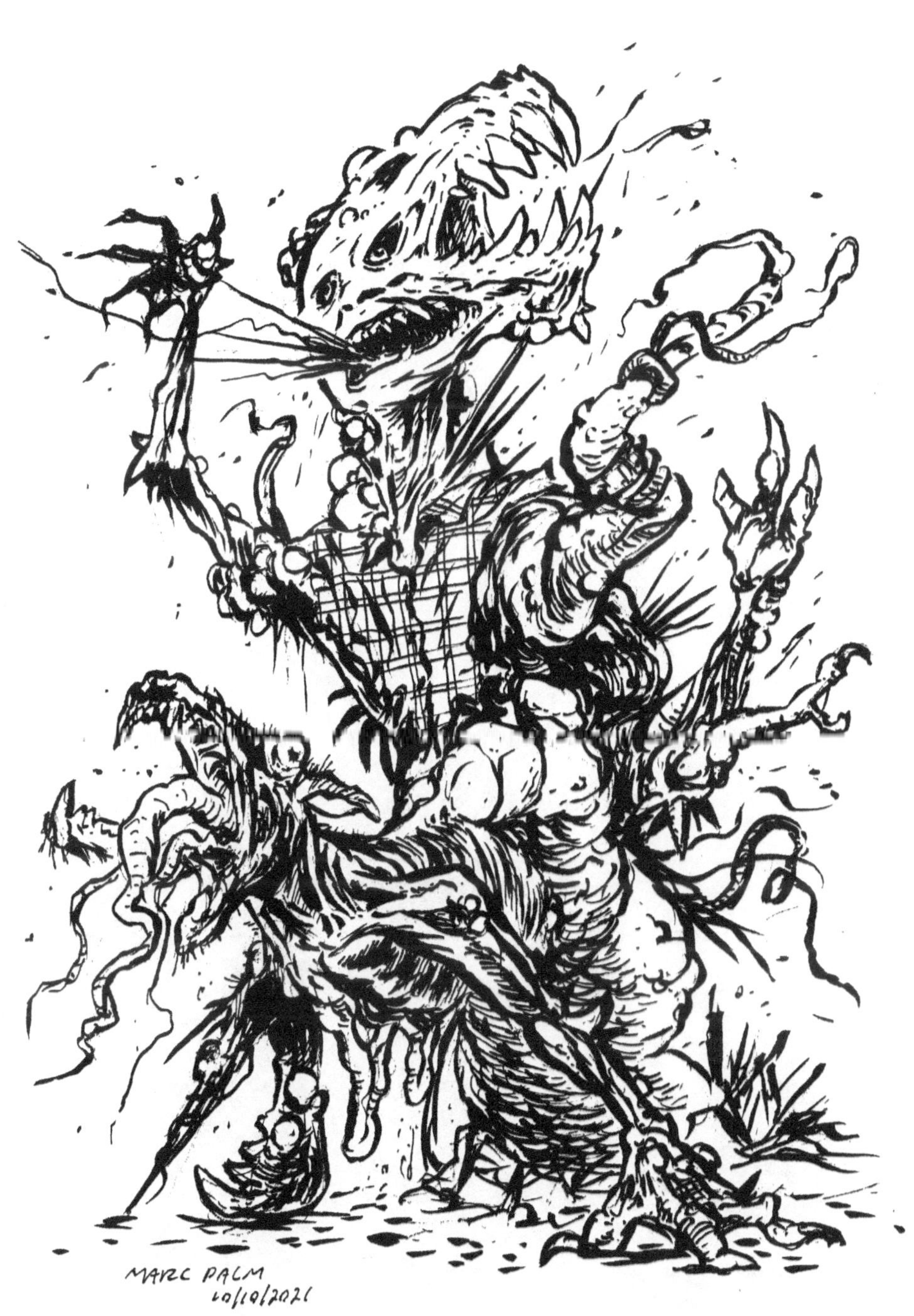
MARC PALM
10/19/2021

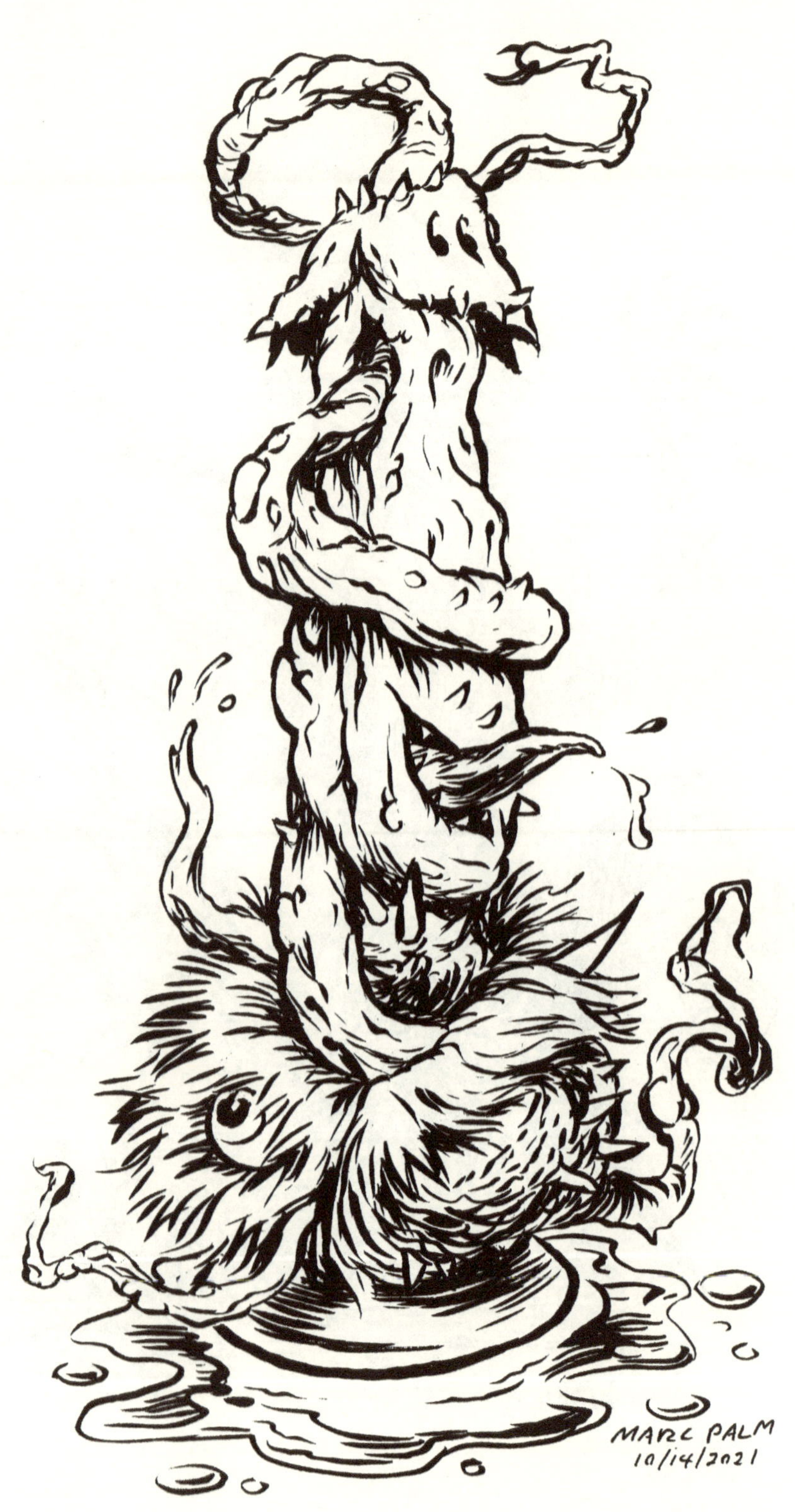
MARC PALM
10/14/2021

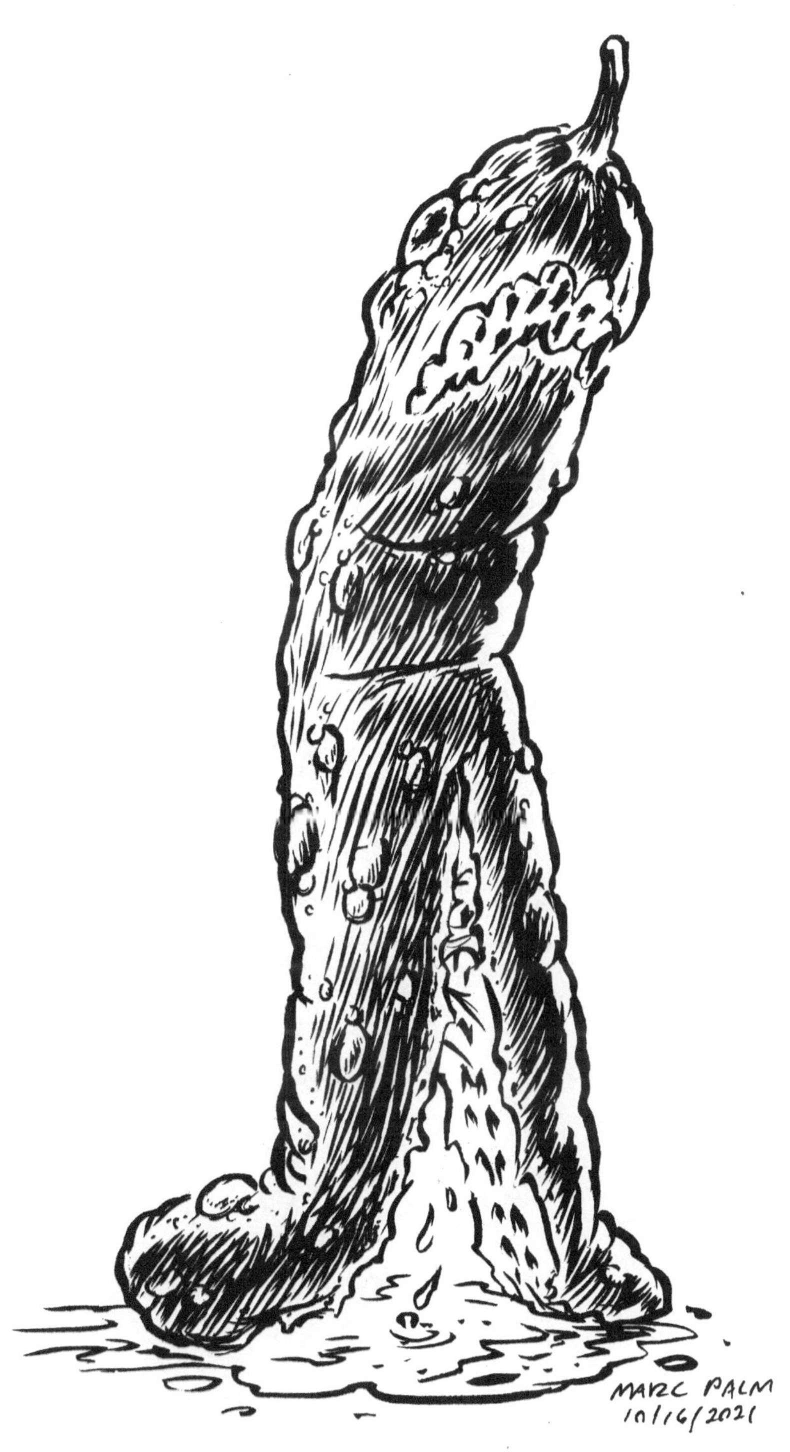

MARC PALM
10/16/2021

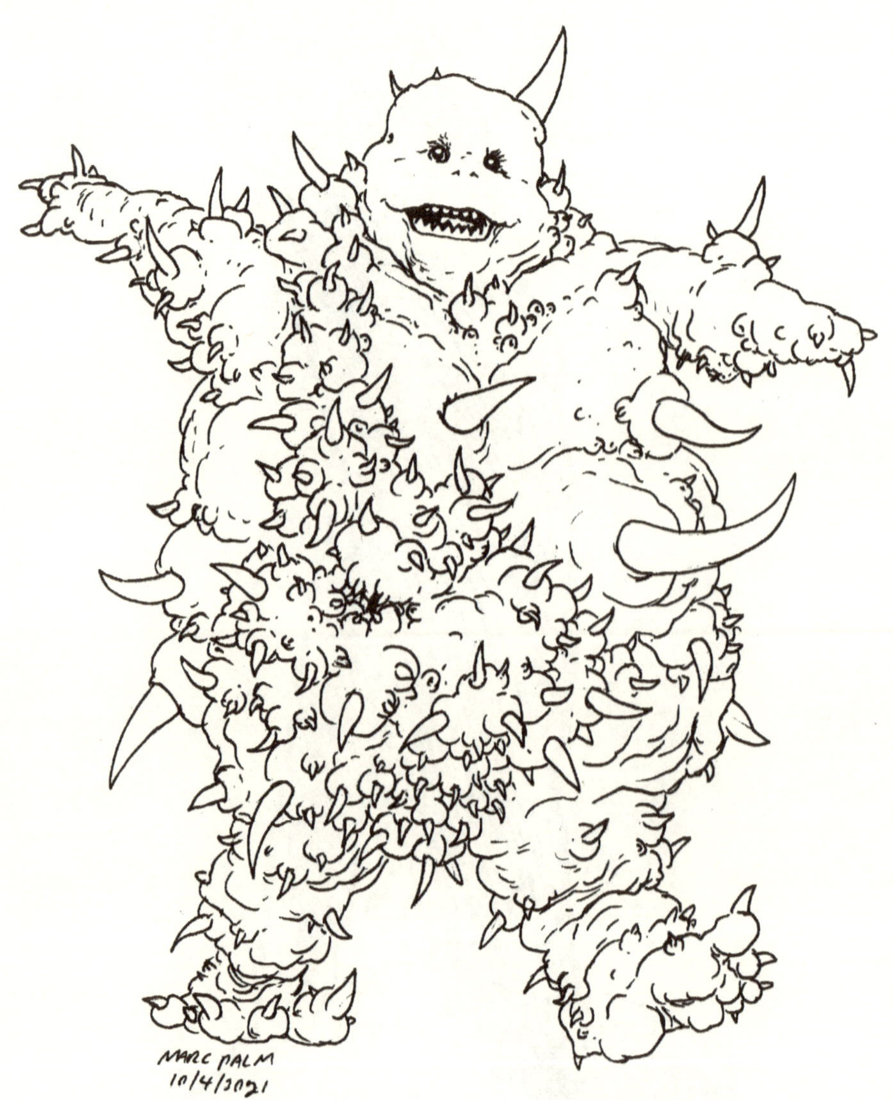

MARC PALM
10/4/2021

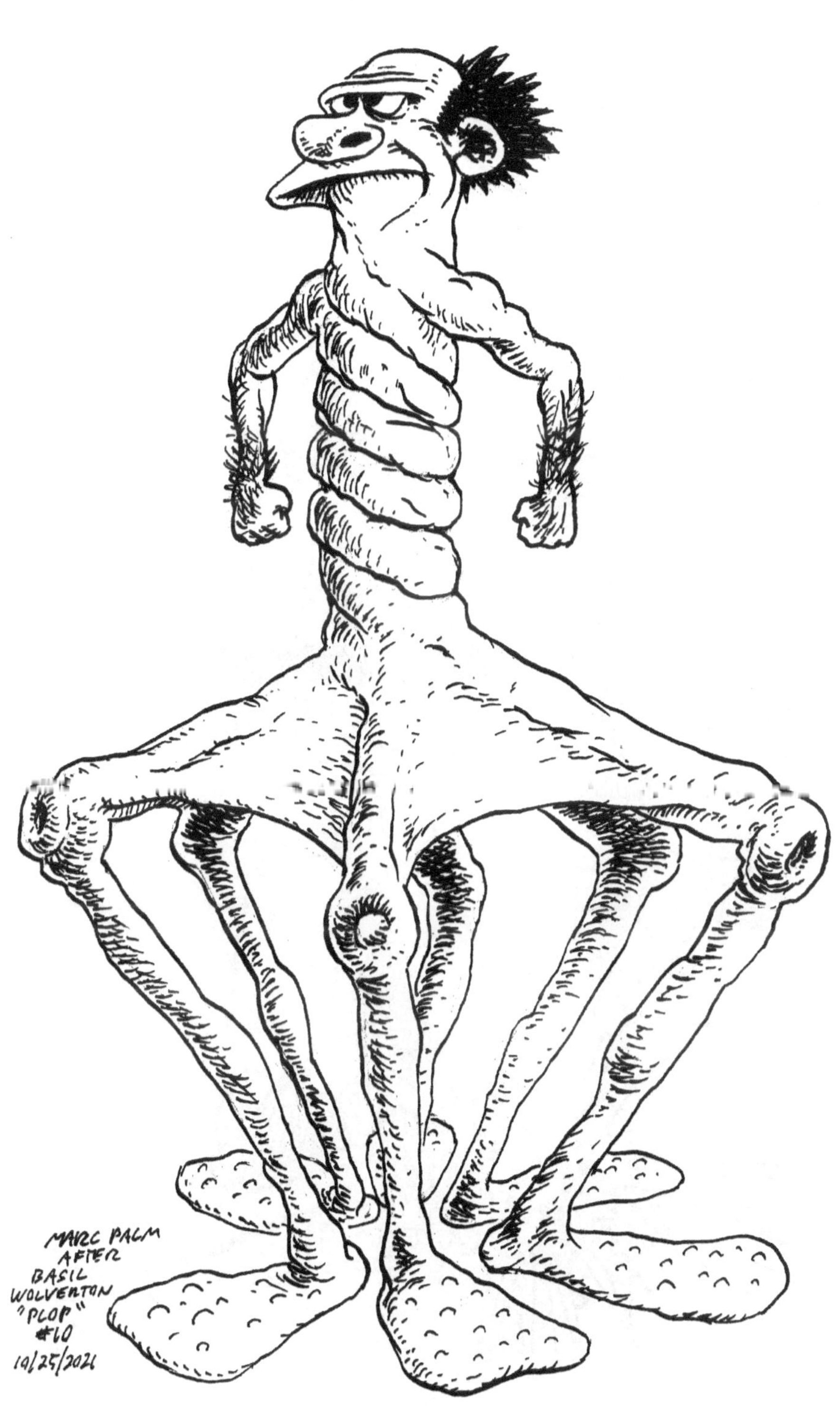

MARC PALM
AFTER
BASIL
WOLVERTON
"PLOP"
#10
10/25/2021

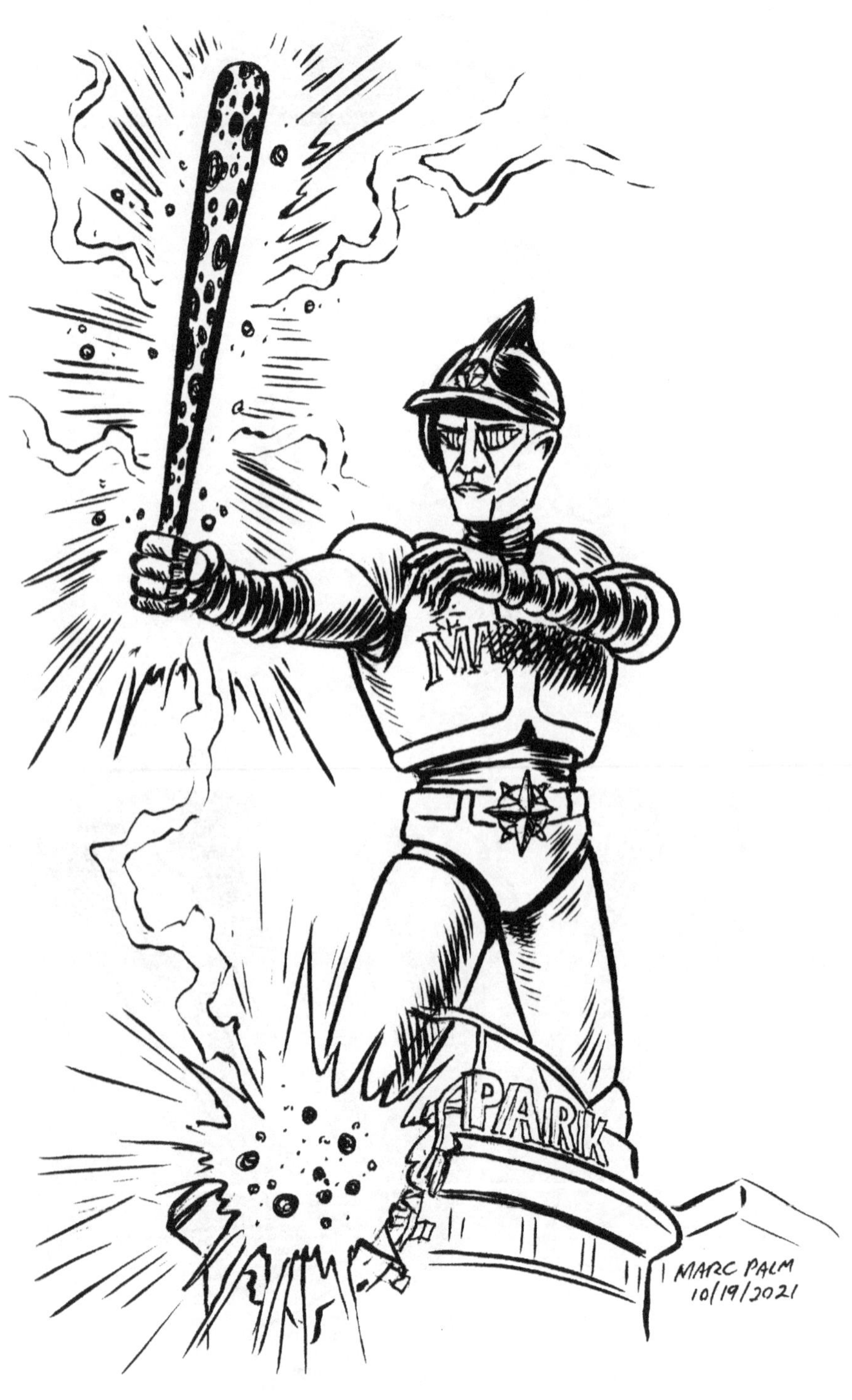
MARINERS
PARK
MARC PALM
10/19/2021

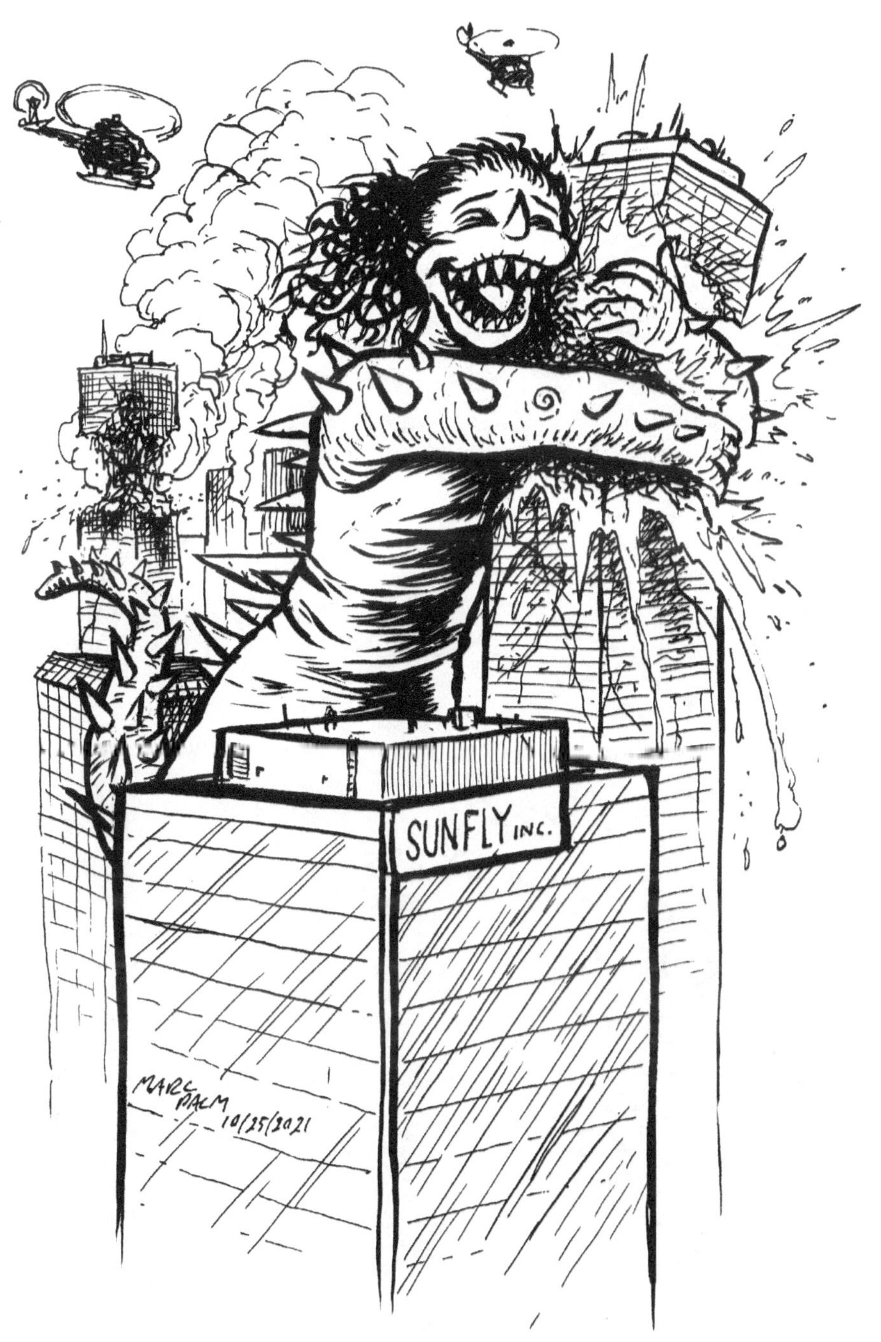

SUNFLY INC.

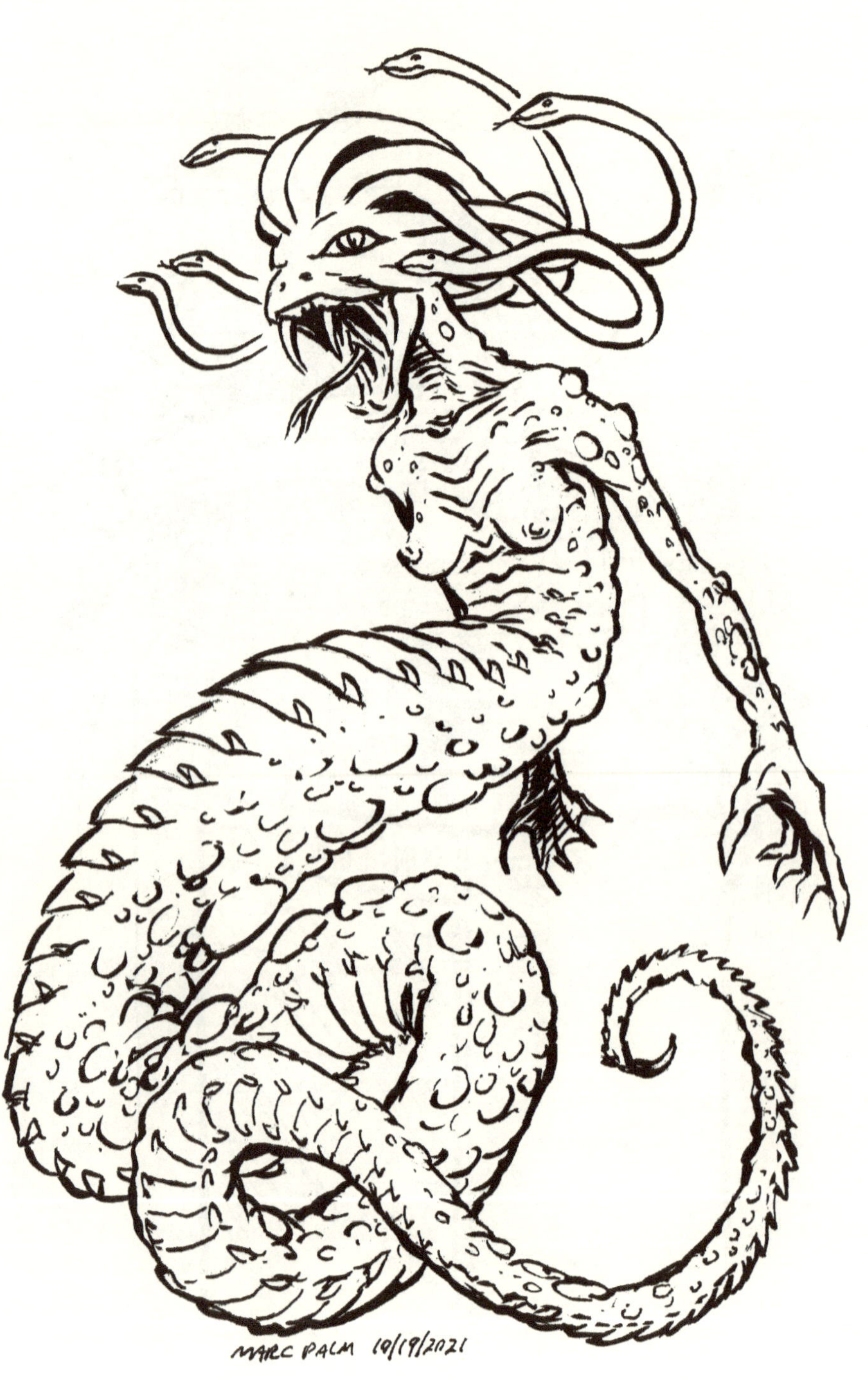
MARC PALM 10/19/2021

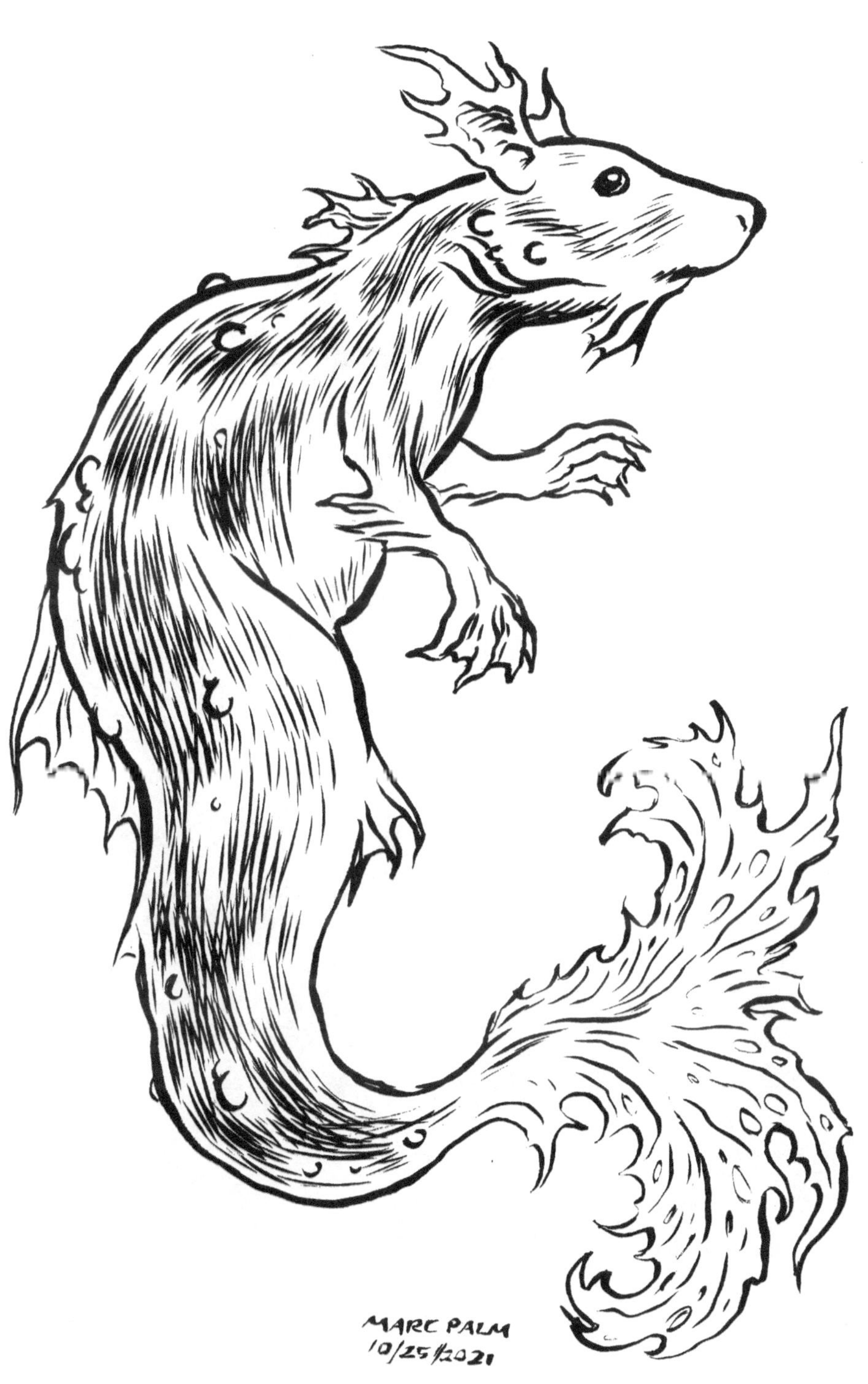

MARC PALM
10/25/2021

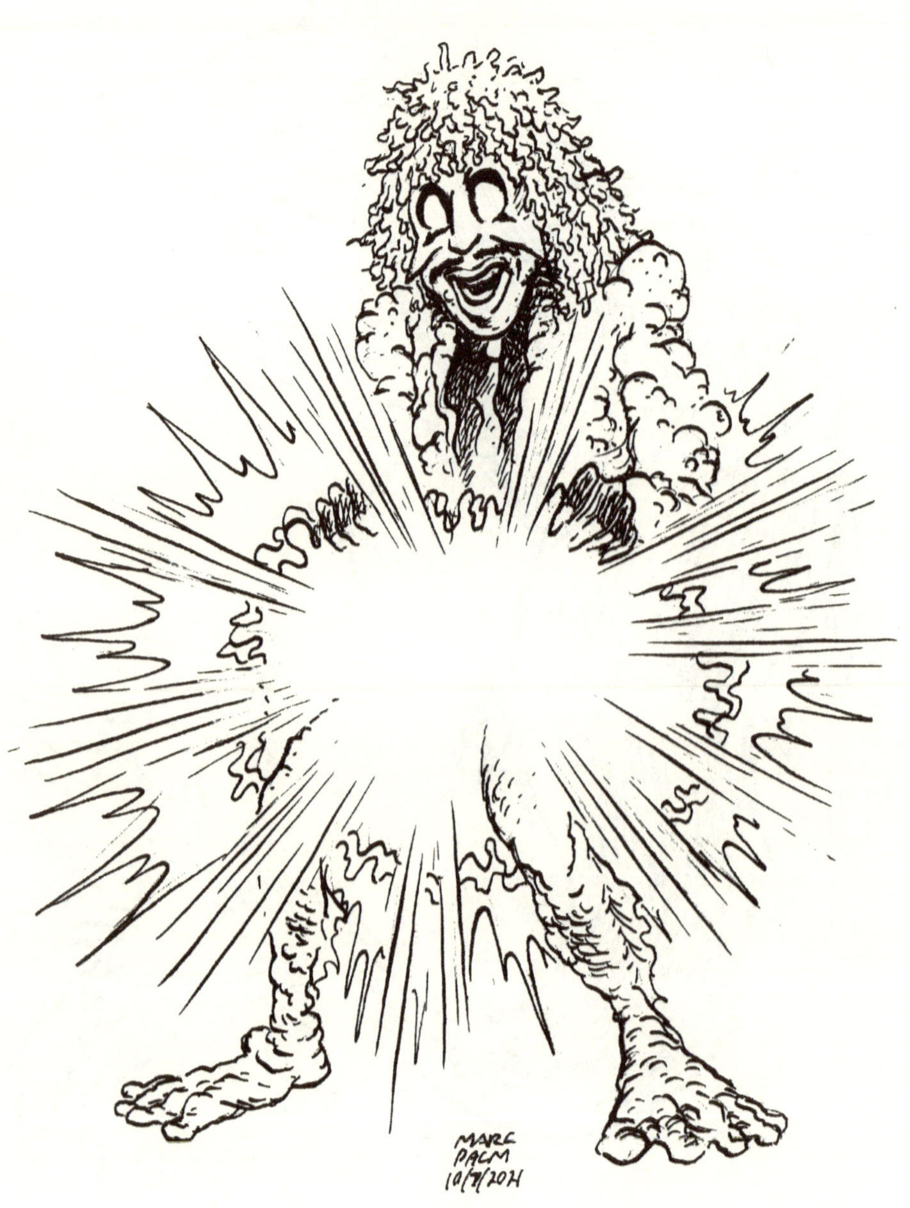
MARC
PACM
10/9/2011

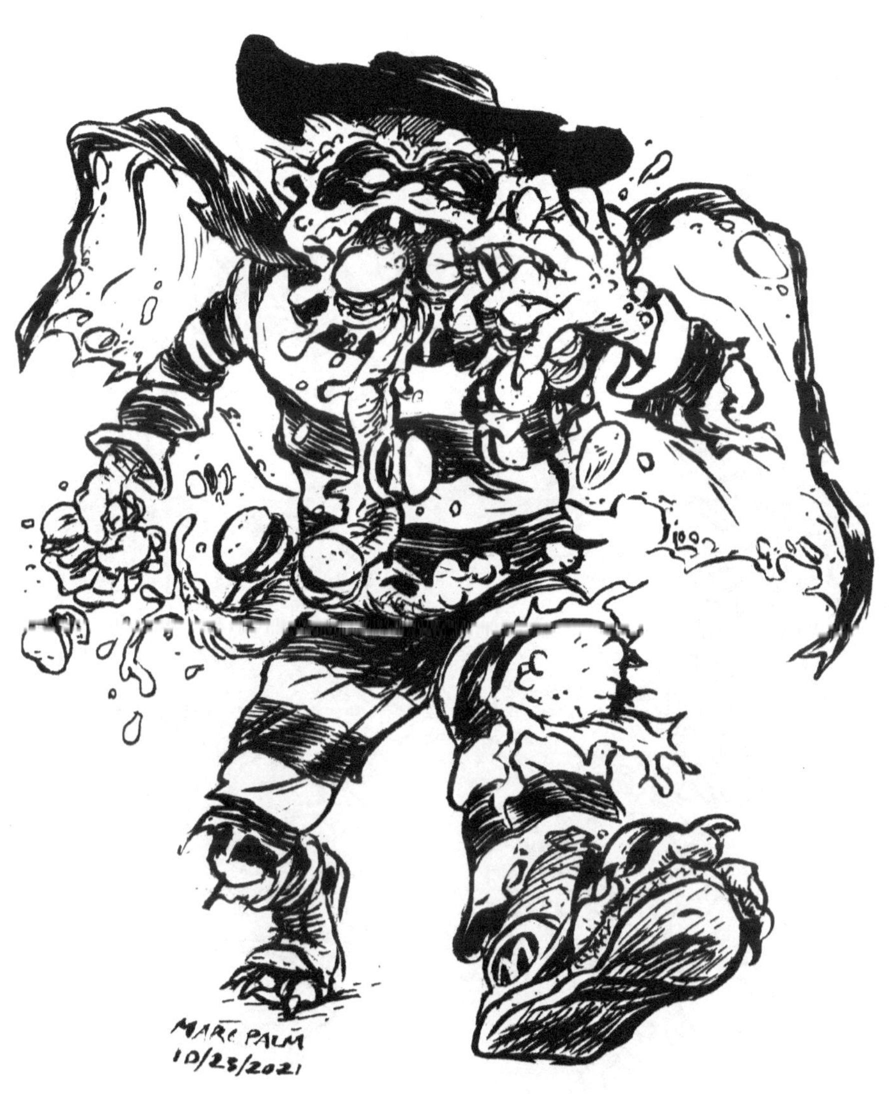

MARC PALM
10/23/2021

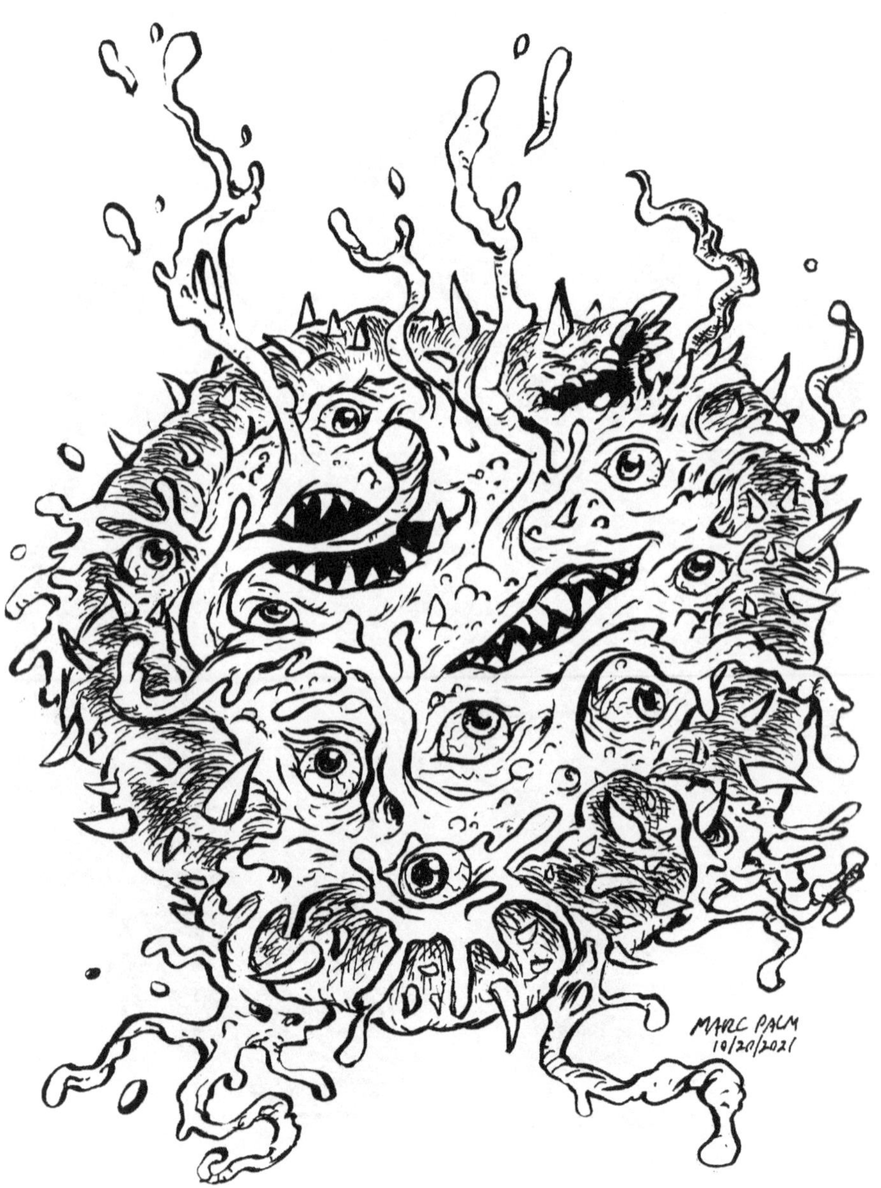
MARC PALM
10/20/2021

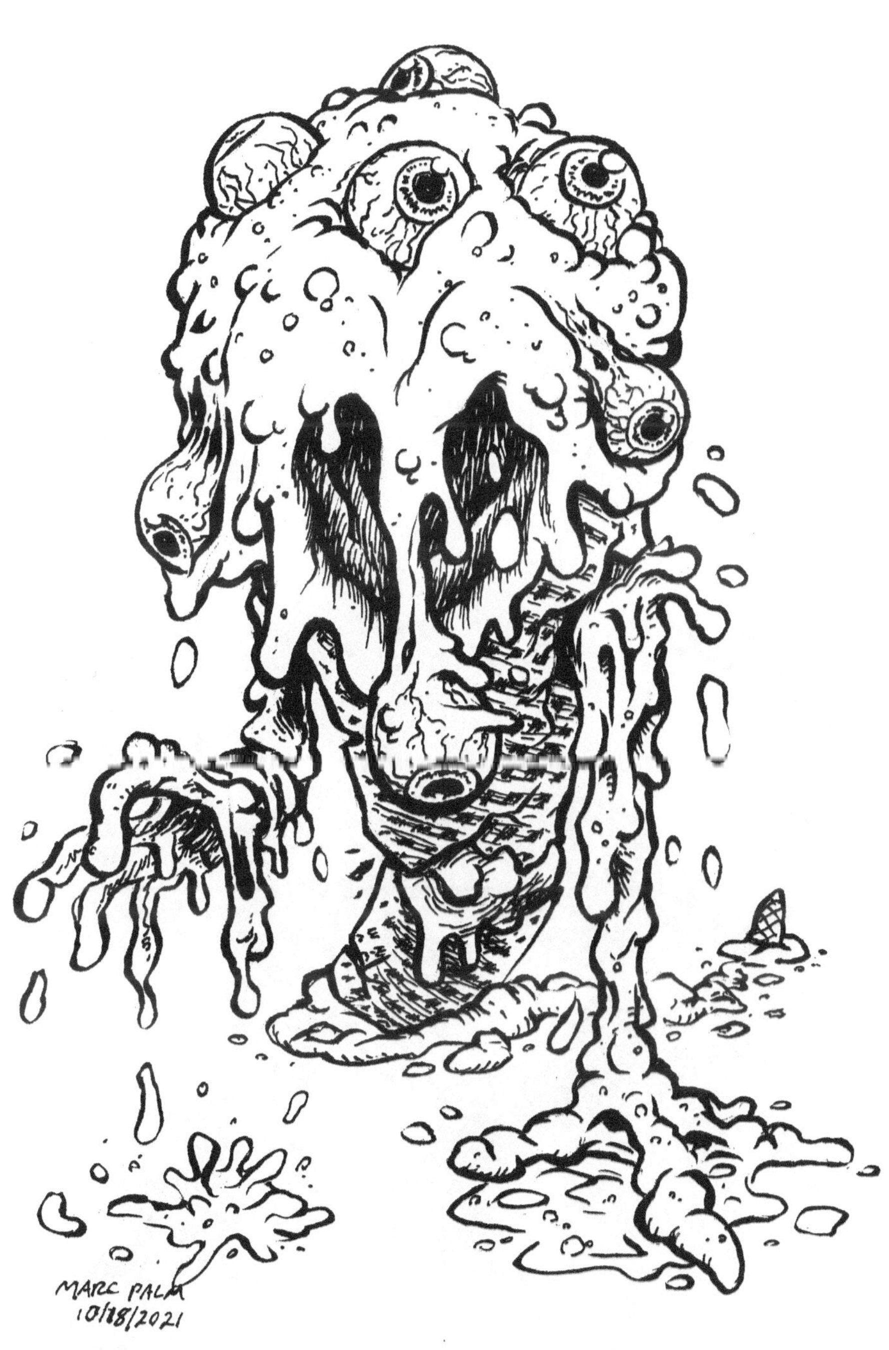
MARC PALM
10/18/2021

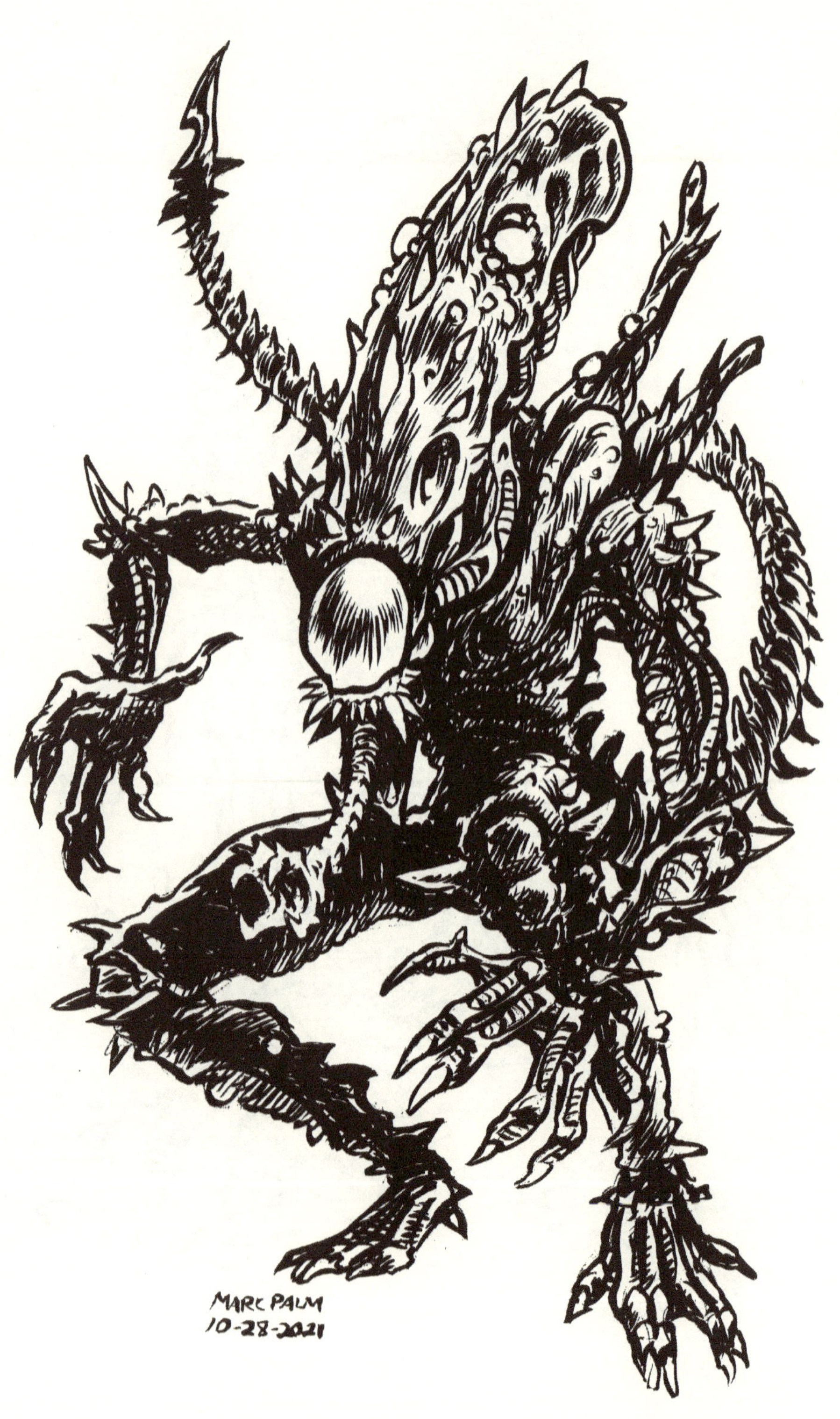
MARC PALM
10-28-2021

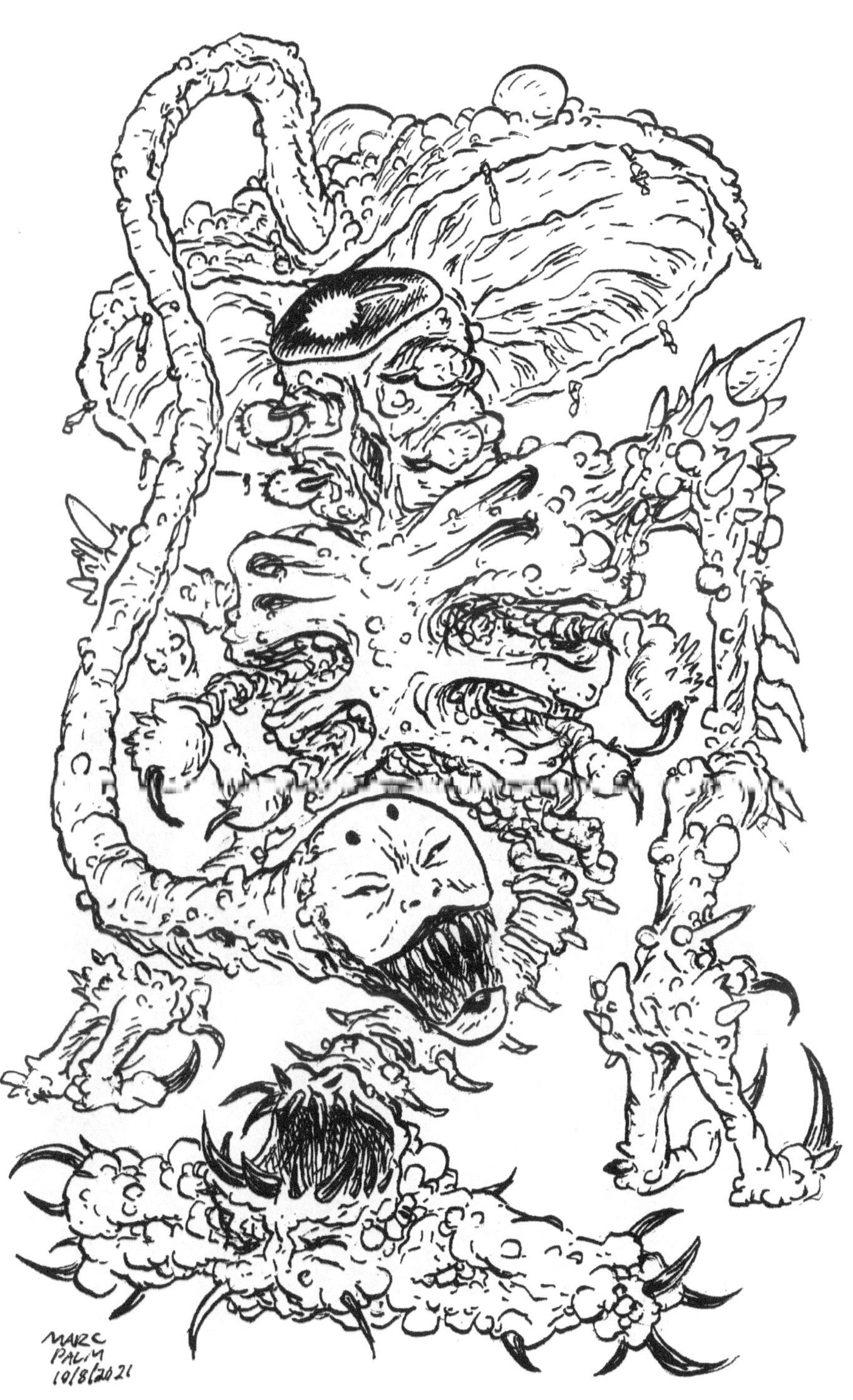

MARC
PALM
10/8/2021

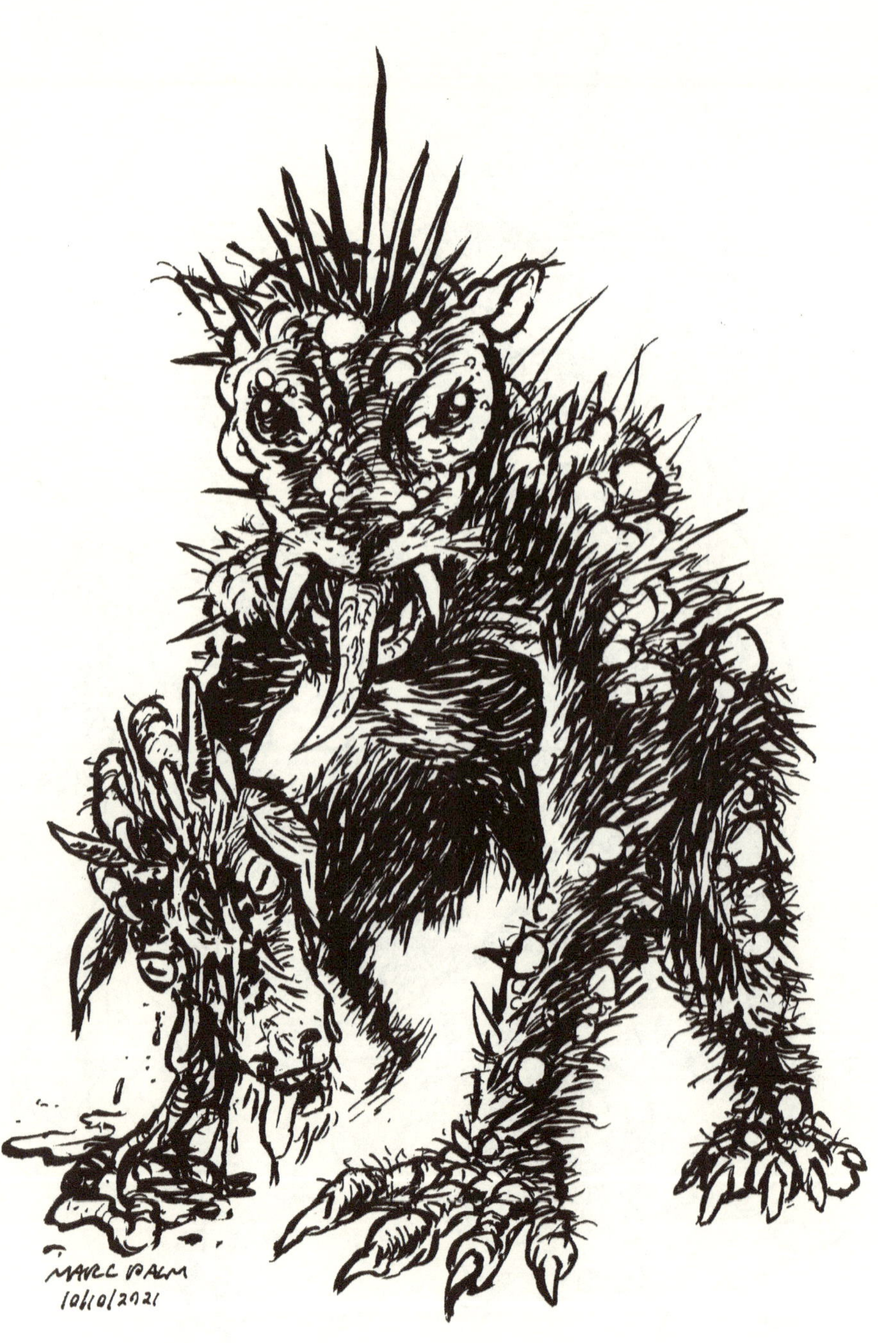

MARC PALM
10/10/2021

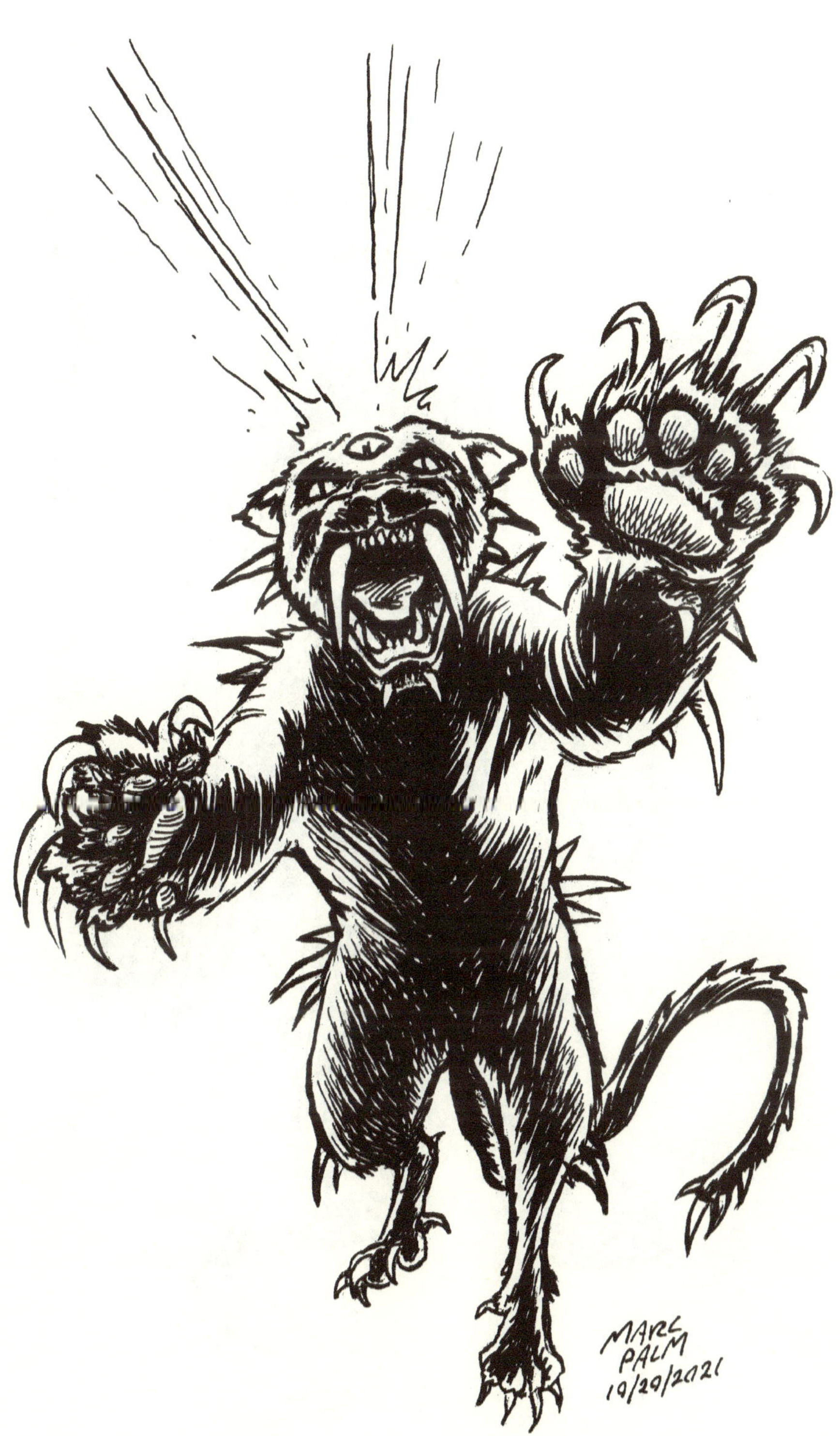

MARC
PALM
10/29/2021

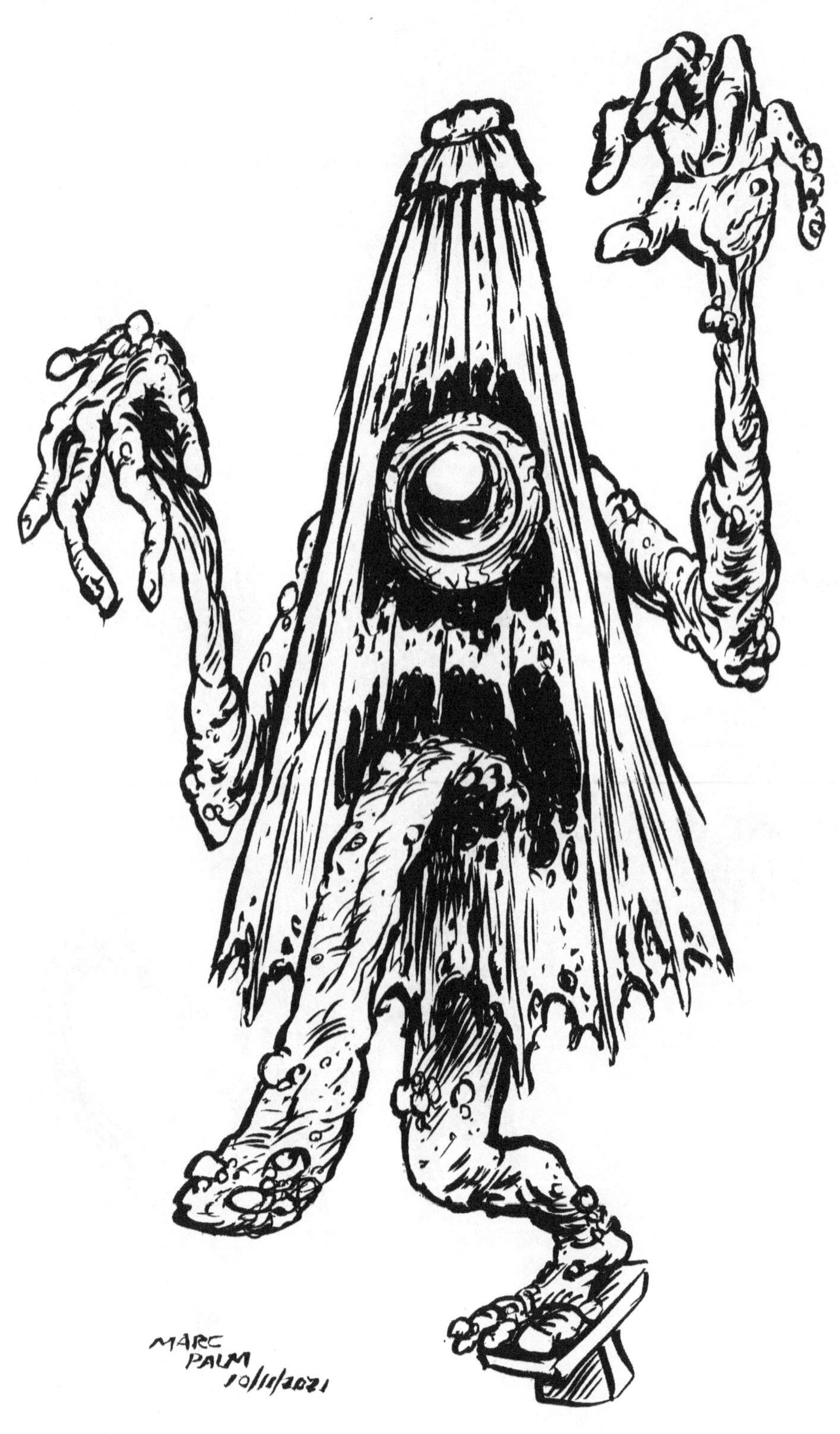
MARC
PALM
10/11/2021

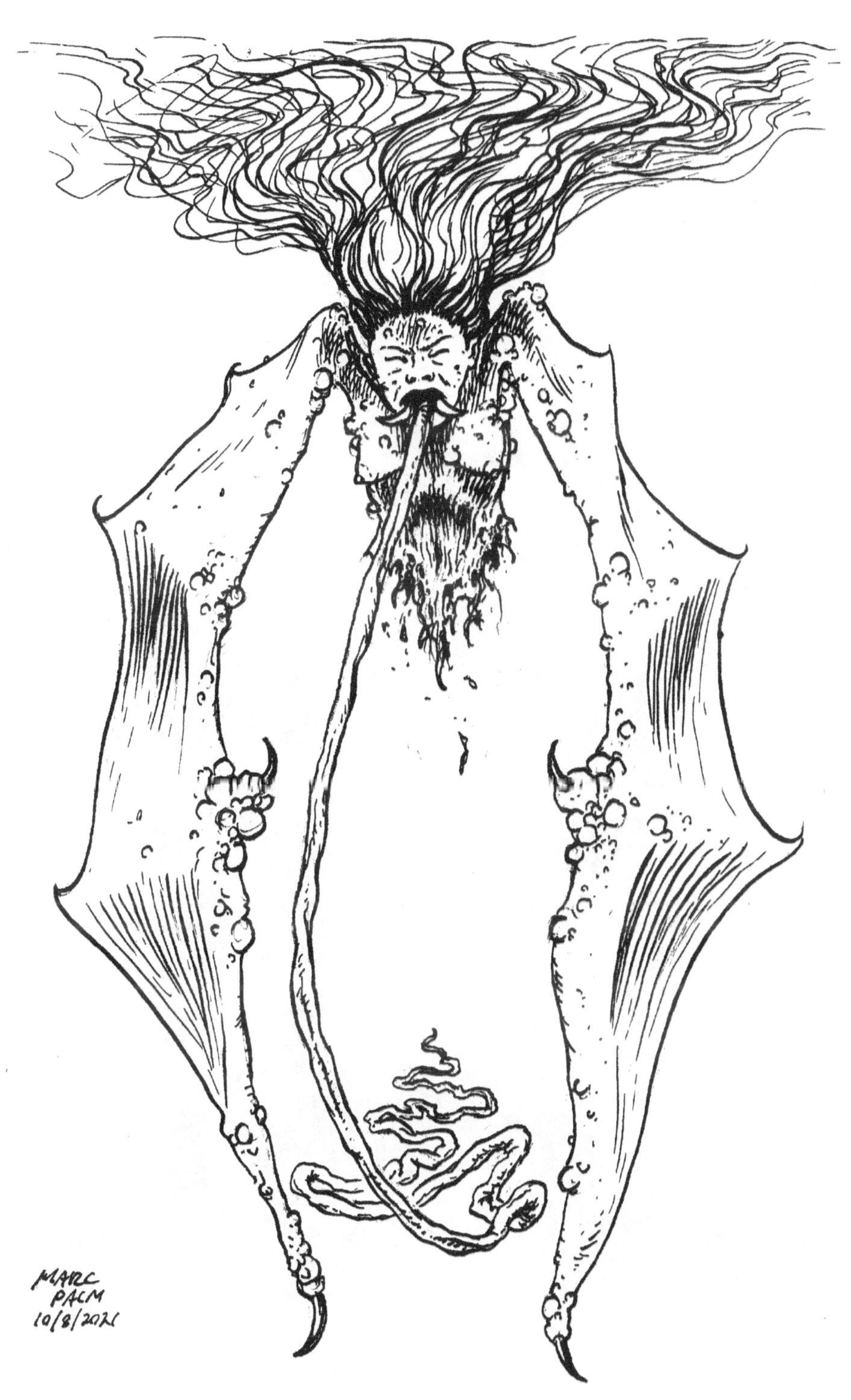
MARC
PALM
10/8/2021

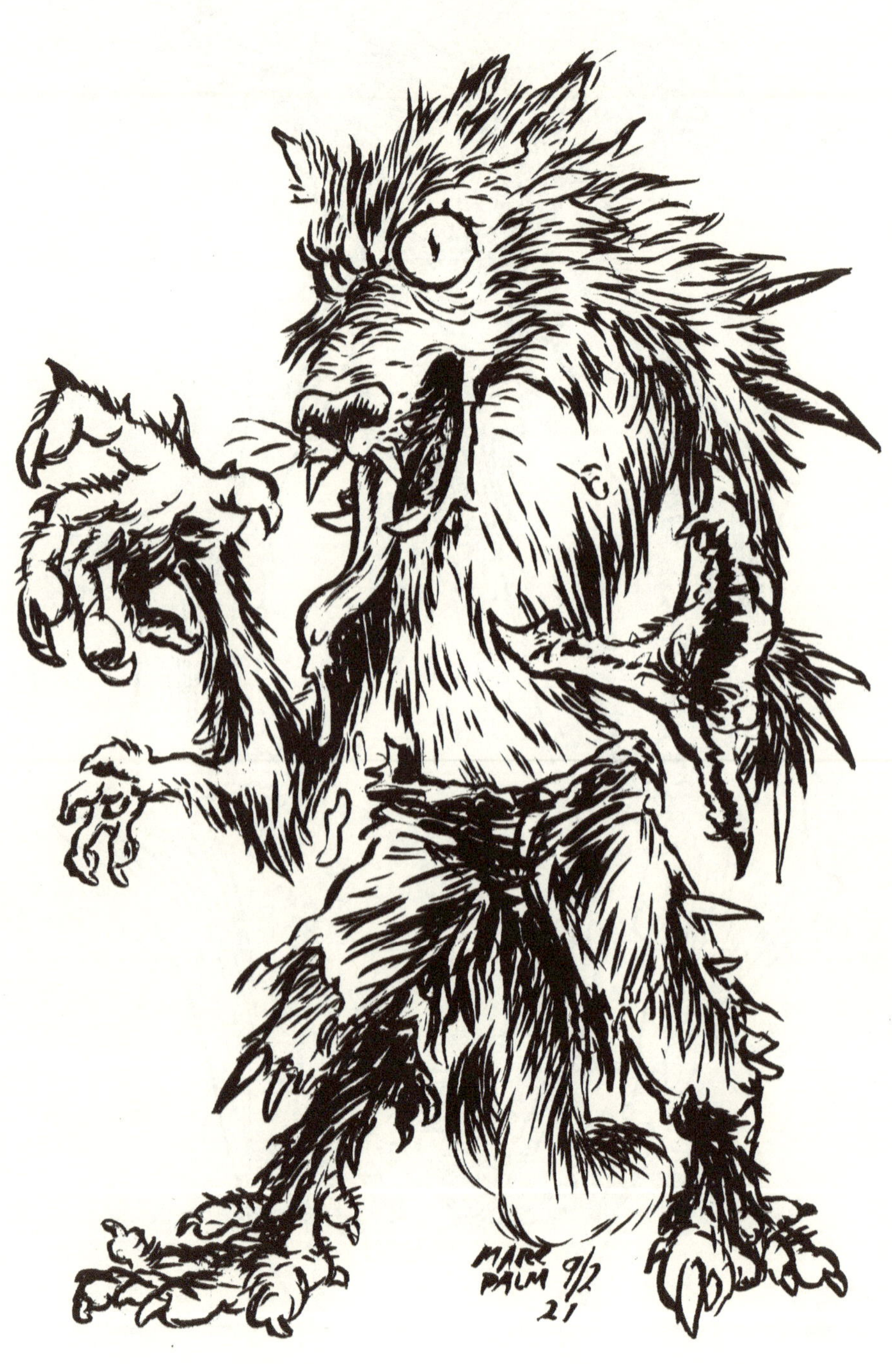
MARC
PALM 9/7
21

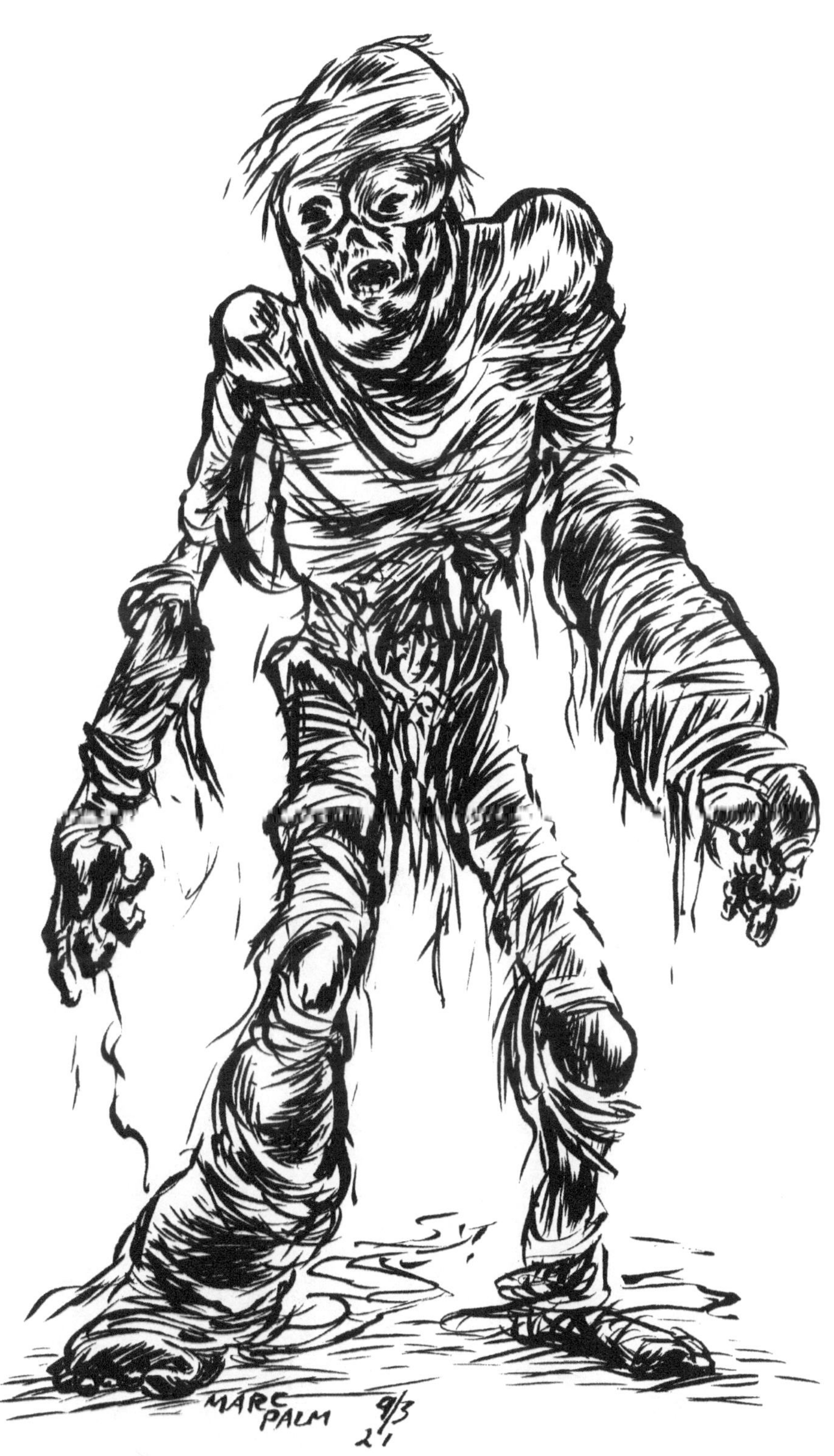

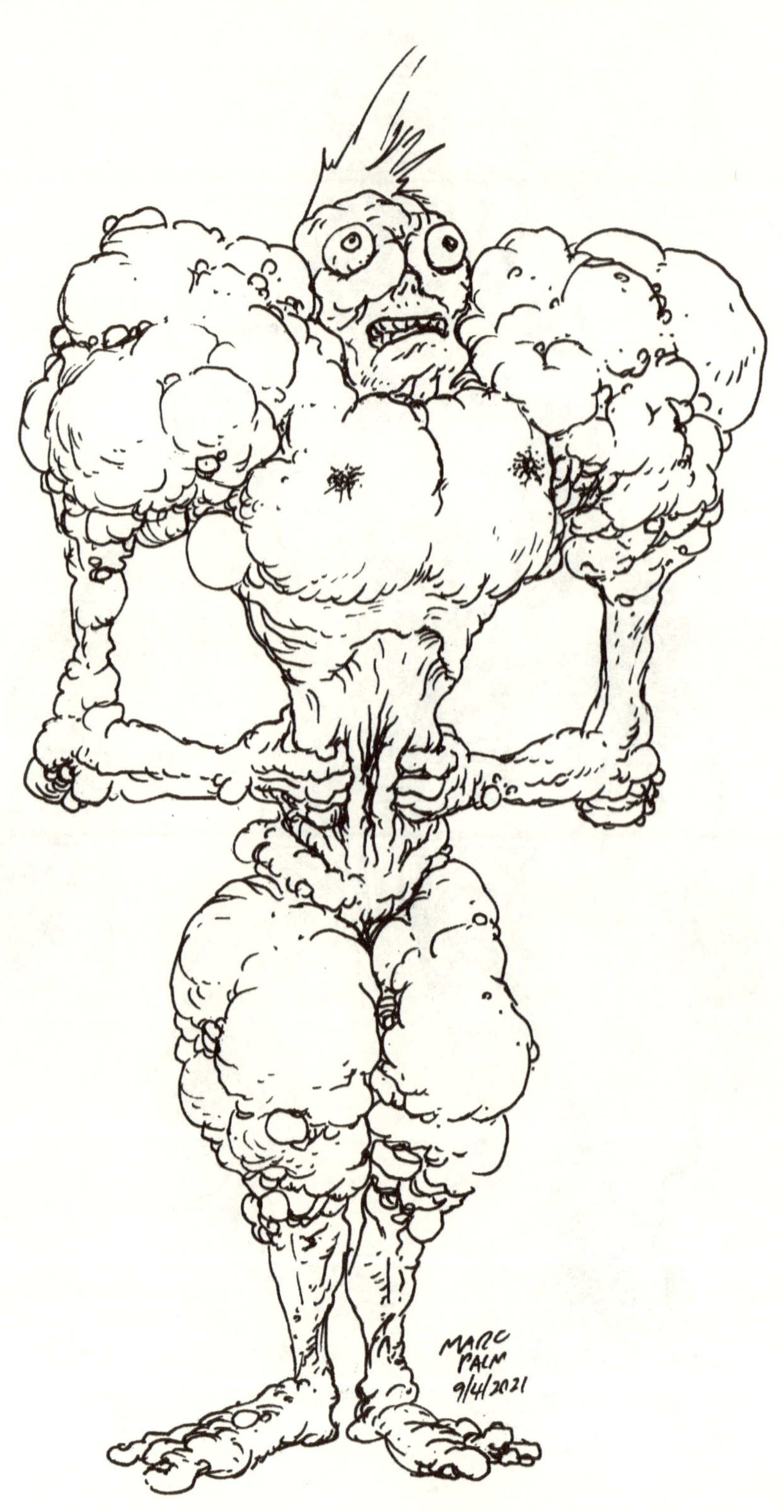

MARC
PALM
9/4/2021

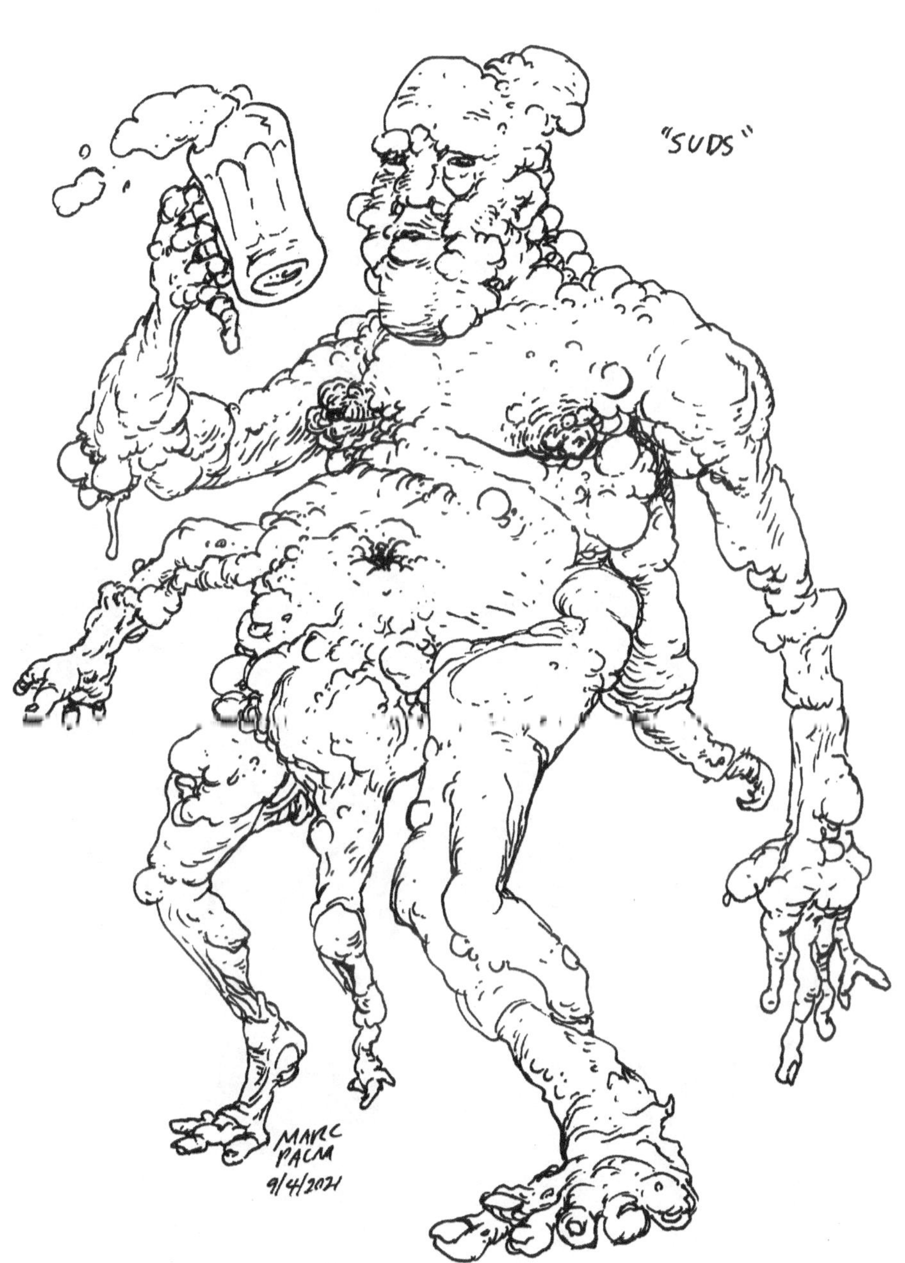

"SUDS"
MARC
PACM
9/4/2021

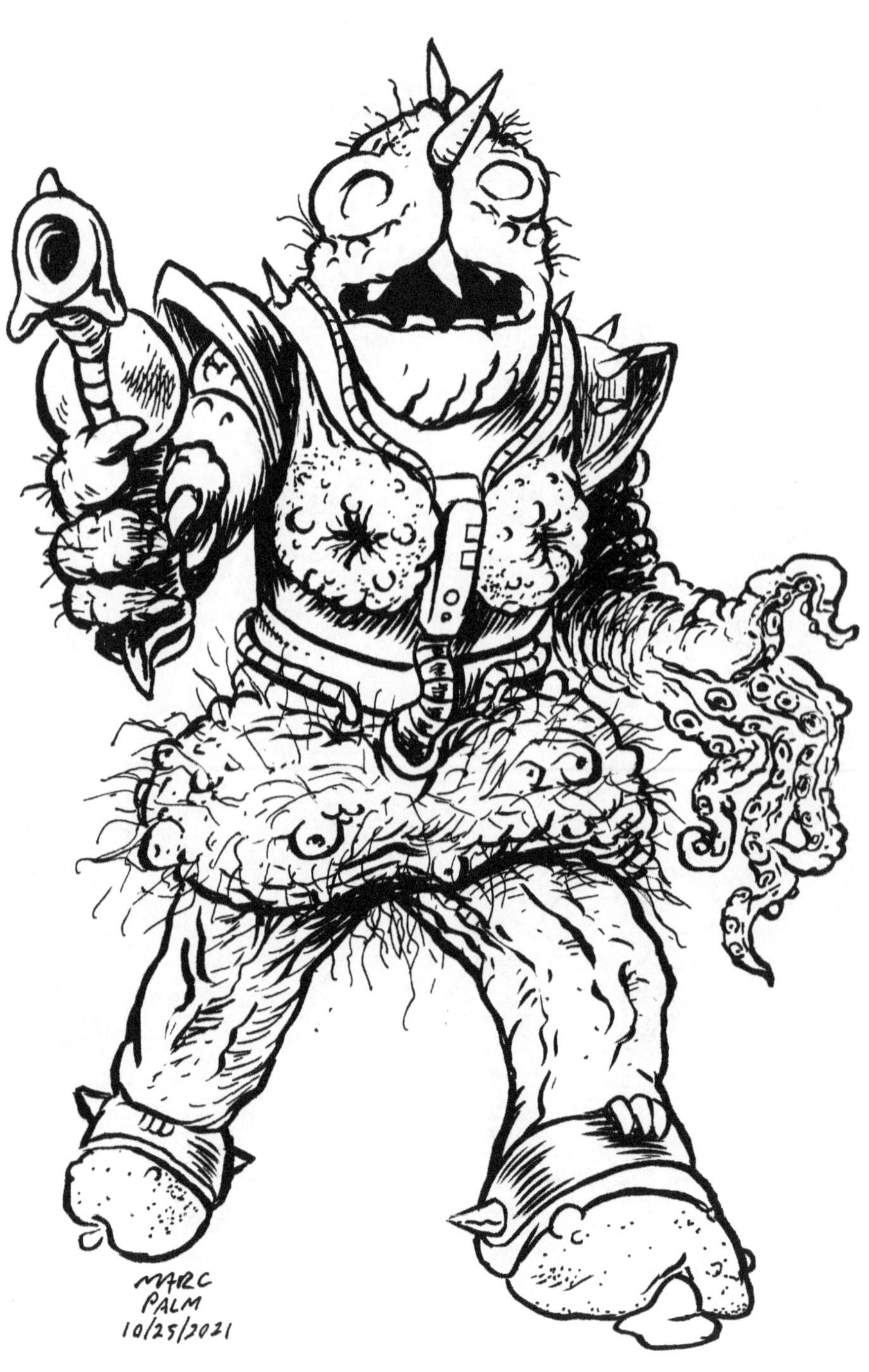

MARC
PALM
10/25/2021

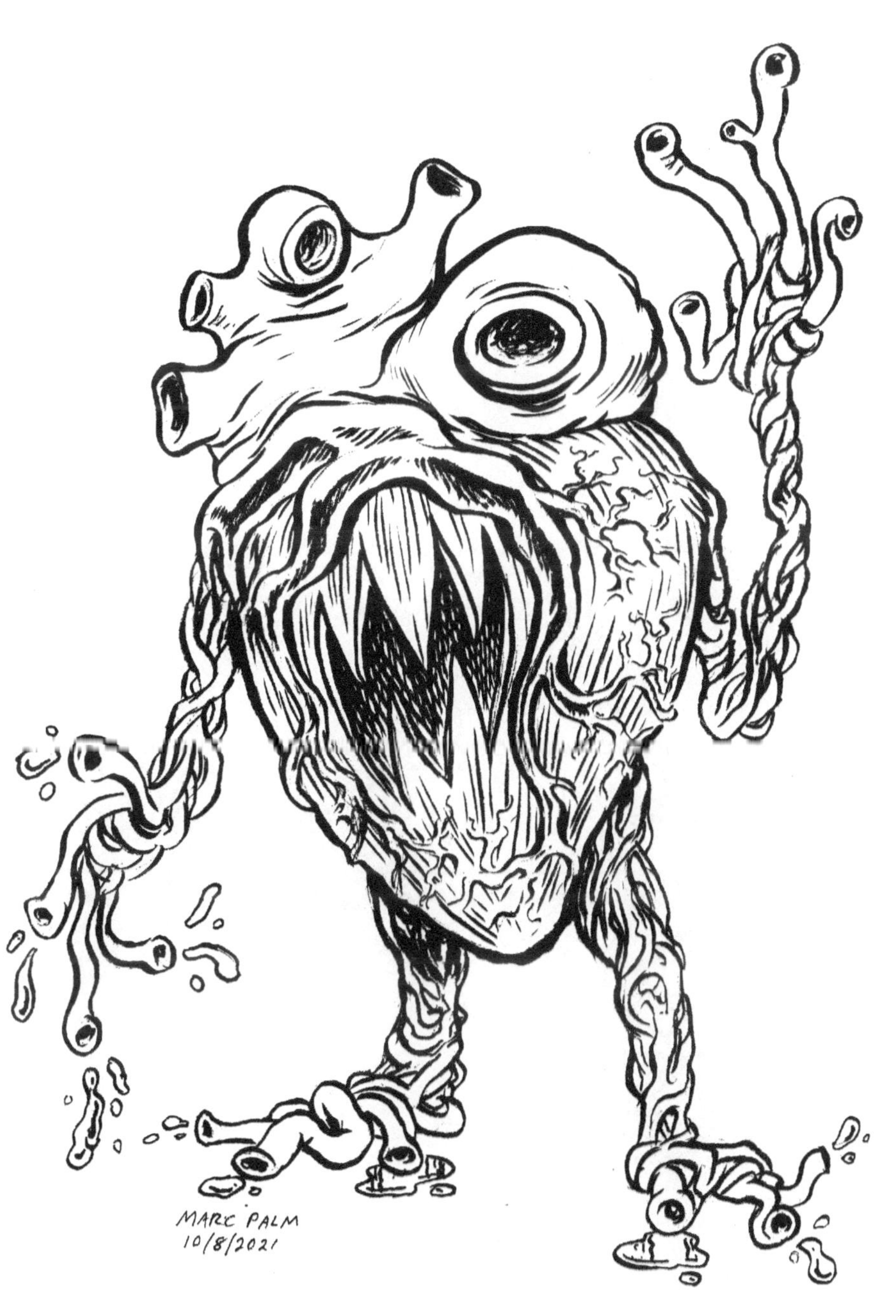

MARC PALM
10/8/2021

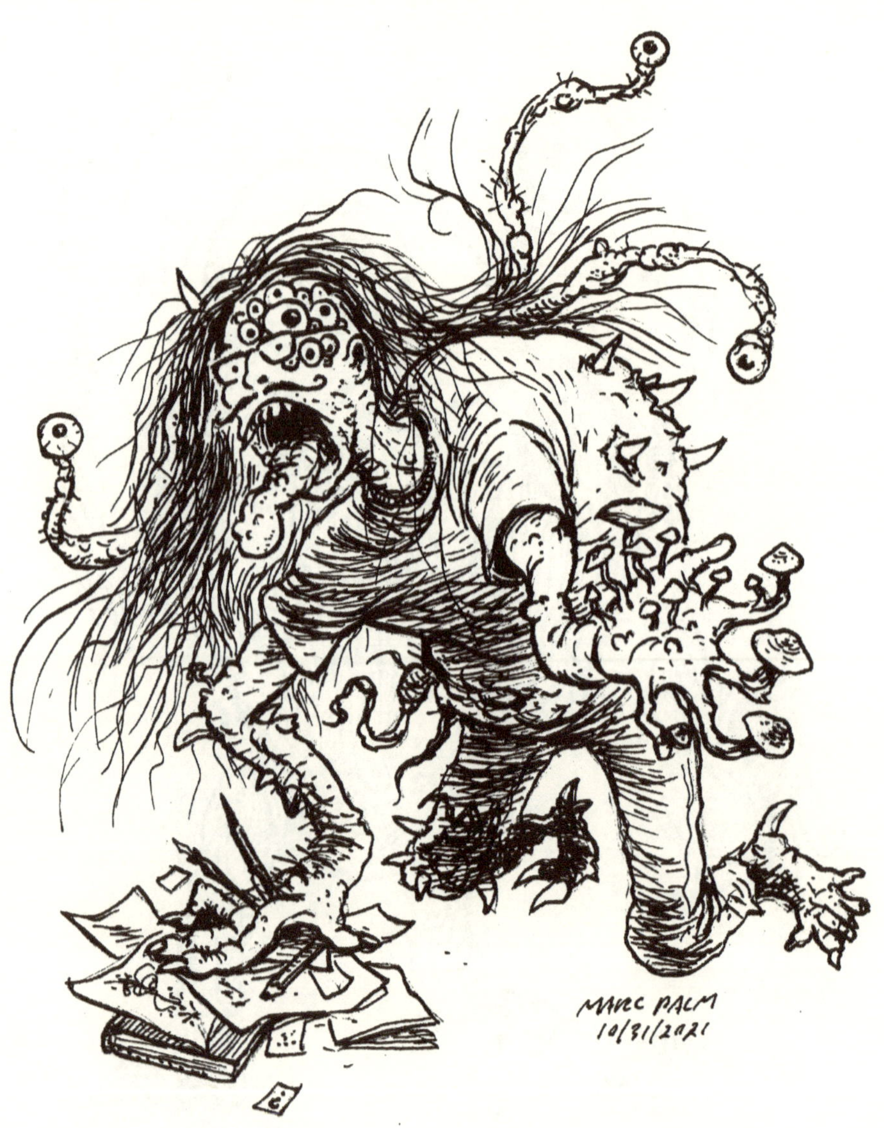

MARC PALM
10/31/2021

www.ingramcontent.com/pod-product-compliance
Lightning Source LLC
Chambersburg PA
CBHW051137250726
48655CB00007B/3110